Promises lovers mak

Women very rarely make promises at the start of a love affair. In fact it is men who say 'We'll always be friends' or who swear eternal love. Why is this? Starting with the motif of the promise, by way of the Brontës, *Four Weddings and a Funeral*, Daphne du Maurier, Nick Leeson and Elizabeth I, psychoanalyst Darian Leader explores the essential questions: Why do people open their mouths when surprised? Why should men often have a compulsion to count things? Why do so many lovers adopt silly baby talk? And why are self-help manuals always less complicated than stereo instructions?

Darian Leader is a psychoanalyst practising in London and in Leeds. He is Senior Lecturer in Psychoanalytic Studies at Leeds Metropolitan University, and was a Founder Member of the Centre for Freudian Analysis and Research in London. He is the author of *Lacan for Beginners* (illustrated by Judy Groves), and *Why do women write more letters than they post?*, which has been translated into twelve languages and received widespread acclaim:

'Beautifully written in an awkward colt-like way, it is unpretentious, individual and rather brave. Leader conjures up a dream-like world where nothing is as it seems, but which has its own weird and unsettling logic.'
Observer

'While most psychoanalytic texts are either dryly academic or banally populist, this one stands out: in exploring new ways of relating myth, fantasy and reality, it follows in the genuine tradition of Freud.'
Financial Times

'If you are invaded by a dreadful feeling of familiarity when reading the title of this book, then rush out and buy it. Darian Leader's study of the sexual relationships between men and women is a positive Pandora's box of embarrassing moments and blush-making sexual *faux pas*, culled exclusively, it seems, from your very own past . . . Thoroughly thought-provoking.' *Marie Claire*

'Leader is urbane and literary, possessed of a range of cultural reference that takes him beyond a narrow circle of initiates. As a writer Leader has considerable charm.' *Independent*

by the same author

LACAN FOR BEGINNERS (with Judy Groves)
WHY DO WOMEN WRITE MORE LETTERS THAN THEY POST?

Promises lovers make when it gets late

DARIAN LEADER

First published in 1997
by Faber and Faber Limited
3 Queen Square London WC1N 3AU
This paperback edition first published in 1998

Typeset by Faber and Faber Ltd
Printed in England by Mackays of Chatham plc, Chatham, Kent

A CIP record for this book
is available from the British Library

ISBN 0-571-19379-X

2 4 6 8 10 9 7 5 3 1

Introduction

The manifesto of a recent self-help book is contained in the sentence, 'Why you should never have sex with a man until you get a commitment from him.' But what might such a commitment actually mean once you've got it? Asking someone else to make a promise is a symptom of doubt, and yet, if you can't rely on a promise, what can you rely on? If words do not offer the ultimate guarantee, what is there instead in the lives of men and women to serve as an anchor? As we will see, where words fail us, something else is put in their place, something to which, without knowing it, we are always more committed than to our real-life partner.

A promise is a statement about the future and its relation to the present. And love, contrary to most other sentiments, is deemed real or illusory depending on how long it lasts. If a man claims to be in love with a woman at breakfast and has forgotten about her by teatime, we usually doubt the authenticity of the emotion. As Jean Cocteau pointed out, the verb 'love' is difficult to conjugate: its past is not simple, its present is not indicative and its future is very conditional.

When we make claims about love, this dimension of time is always evoked. And when we make love, however much we may want to make time stand still, each gesture of the body may become a sign of the future. When H. G. Wells kissed Rebecca West for the first time, she wanted to know what the kiss meant, what it promised. If H. G. liked the idea of pure animal passion, Rebecca's concern showed the impossibility of her partner's dream: each kiss, each caress, each contact was both a sensation *and* a sign of what lay ahead. As we explore the theme of promises, we are led naturally to this problem of expectations: why we look with hope to the future, how we forget the past and what, finally, it means to be late – both sexually and socially.

There are many psychoanalytic ideas in this book, mostly derived from Freud and Lacan, and spiced with the observations of Theodor Reik, a student of Freud whose books continue to sparkle with ingenuity and insight. I have also given a special place to the work of Helene Deutsch and Edmund Bergler: although their papers and books lack the neological disguise which often seems necessary today in psychoanalytic literature, anyone interested in psychoanalysis may read them with profit, and hopefully abandon the common vision of the work of Freud's students as merely a repository of all the errors of the past. Contrary to what many people think, the mind is still far from being understood, and what we read in the media about its functioning would often be better communicated in a fairground booth. Freud's ideas were developed and refined by Jacques Lacan, and his work provides a programme of research which is rich in its implications and powerful in its logic. It is easier, of course, to reject the findings of psychoanalysis wholesale than to take them seriously, and sadly not much can be done about that. Rebecca West once said that 'chattering in favour of psychoanalysis is, heaven knows, a habit that is silly enough, but chattering against it seems to make those who do it sillier still'. Since no one wants to be silly, I hope that they will read this book in a Westian way, and suspend, for a moment, their contempt for 'what happens by chance to be imported from France'.

Many friends and colleagues have contributed to the contents of this book, and I would like to thank Isolde Barker-

Mill, Alain de Botton, Marie-Laure Bromley-Davenport, Bernard Burgoyne, Helen Chaloner, David Corfield, Judy Groves, Alison Hall, Diggory Kenrick, Simone Meentzen, Gretel Mitchell, Maria Olsson, Joe O'Neill, Esther Palacios, Jennifer Scanlon, Sally Singer, Vikki Smith, Silvia Tendlarz, Stephanie Theobald, Natasha Walter and Christine Wertheim. I have made frequent use of the biographies of Daphne du Maurier by Margaret Forster and Judith Cook, and have learnt much from Walter Burkert's work on classical civilization. Geneviève Morel's investigations of female sexuality have been particularly enlightening, and I would like to thank her for providing so much inspiration in this difficult and delicate field of research. I am also grateful to Simon Gunn and Eric Roper at Leeds Metropolitan University for their support. At Faber I have benefited as always from the careful criticism of Julian Loose, and at Simpson Fox from the enthusiasm and encouragement of Georgina Capel. I hope that all of the above find that this book reflects, in one way or another, what they have contributed to it.

One

In scary films, people say 'I'll be right back', and they're usually wrong. In beds, people say 'I'll always love you' or 'I'll always be faithful to you', and they're usually wrong too. How and why they're wrong is one of the things this book is about. Rather than simply asking why we fall in love, it is thus a question of asking why love doesn't always last forever. Love may be slow in its beginnings, but it is often swift in its endings, and the qualities which were once most cherished in the partner may become those which are the most despised. And if love is more likely to twist into hate than into indifference, why the strange proximity of love and hate? Why is it that one of these sentiments will always surface in exactly the place where we would expect the other?

The promises lovers make can tell us something about these questions, and about the different conceptions of the future that each of us holds. If it is true that most people's lives consist mainly of the expectation of things to come, a promise might seem like a blessing, but at its horizon is more often a farewell than a future.

Speaking about the unsettled nature of her affections, a woman describes how she had left her long-term partner to travel back to the city of her childhood. Within days she has moved in with another man and when he asks for her hand in marriage, she accepts unconditionally. Yet she feels compelled all the same to tell her first lover of this decision in person. When she arrives on a Friday, she stays in his bed until Monday morning, and knows that this is the man she won't leave. What makes her return to the second man, she says, is something very precise: she had made a promise to marry, and this promise had to be honoured. After the marriage, she felt relief and it was now possible to divorce: her feelings of guilt evaporated and she was no longer burdened by the obligation of her vow. The promise here had not been offered spontaneously by the woman, as the man had asked her at the start to say Yes, a detail which illustrates the way in which men so often make or demand promises about beginning relationships, while women perhaps are more likely to make promises about ending them. As she embraced her first lover, although she knew she would honour her word and marry the second, she made one further promise, though this time a silent one: to leave her betrothed once he had become her husband. If the man had demanded a promise about the start of a relationship from a woman, it was now the woman who made a promise about the end of a relationship, not to a man but to herself.

What is interesting in this example is that the conscious feelings of guilt were removed rather than accentuated by the divorce, and although she admitted a certain fondness for the husband, she was untroubled by the thought of leaving him. In contrast, it happens from time to time that a woman feels guilty if a man confesses his love to her and she can neither say Yes to his proposals nor love him back, a situation which may produce a strange gravitation towards the same man. Although she has rejected him, she is drawn to him. One might choose to explain this with the observation that a woman may feel responsible for the man's loving her, as if, being the cause herself, she must bear the effects on her own shoulders: if it wasn't for her, the man wouldn't love her. There may also be moments at which disowning a very real desire for the man in question generates the guilty feeling, or simply the thought of having an illicit relationship, regardless of the man's identity. But as another woman who had rejected a man put it, what made her so attached to him was the haunting image of the rejected suitor: each time she thought about him, it was this image that kept coming back. And as she elaborated the many scenes of her childhood in which she had been excluded in some way, it became clear to her that this rejected man was herself: if her rejection of him had set up the identity, she was now pushed towards him as if to her own image.

If it is true that women very rarely make promises at the start of a love affair, this prudence must have its reasons. In *A Midsummer Night's Dream*, Hermia pledges to be at her rendezvous 'by all the vows that ever men have broke, in number more than ever women spoke'. In popular wisdom, men make promises about love in order to obtain sex, but today they may promise before, during and after. Many years ago, such promises formed part of the marriage contract itself, but today, without this legal agenda, it is a question why they turn up with such frequency. And if promising appeals to love and devotion, the relation to sex becomes complicated since love and sex are not the same thing. There is no less truth than humour in Theodor Reik's observation that love and sex are like whisky and soda: you only confuse them once you've had too much. When you wake up, the difference between them becomes sharper, but it is a fact that men and women wake up, and go to sleep, at different times. A man will often call a woman late at night, as he lies alone in his room, but a woman is more likely to think of a man in this way in the morning, perhaps thinking about whether she will be included in his schedule. Their relations to love, to sex and to time are not the same. Poets used to say that love is a dream, with the implication that since dreams have endings, so do love affairs. Endings, of course, suppose beginnings and we will see how the way in which love ends can be reflected in the way it starts: what lovers promise early on may tell us something about what will happen to them when it gets late. The two privileged moments of the promise are, after all, at the start of a relationship and then, in desperation, at its end.

A woman complained of her injured feelings whenever a man failed to vow his love to her, yet added that she became even more nervous if he did: the suspicions at the man's silence were only multiplied once he spoke. Promises, after all, introduce the possibility of their being broken, which was not there before they were. And if this possibility can disenchant, why promise at the start of a relationship, unless you are unsure that you will perform what you promise?

Many self-help books advise their readers to obtain not just one but a whole set of promises from the person with whom they are considering sharing their life or sleeping with. According to one popular volume, these promises should be obtained in daylight and not during a petting situation, possibly to avoid the situation so frequent in Restoration comedies where one party enters an agreement with another, deceived as to the latter's identity due to the poor visibility of the surroundings. In Aphra Behn's play *The Lucky Chance*, Bearjest thinks that he is marrying the heiress Diana yet ends up binding himself to a servant due to the poor lighting conditions. If modern self-help books had been more readily available, perhaps he would have got the heiress, but one may still suspect that neither printed advice nor electricity would have been enough to avert the errors of his passion. Whether they are made in daylight or not, the promises these volumes instruct are not the answer to the problems of lovers. As we shall see, voicing a commitment might be both the cause and the symptom of a variety of discomforts. If you feel confident enough to follow the instructions of self-help books with your lover, rather than making any promises it may be less unfortunate to turn to the older method of appeasement and read the texts aloud to one another. In this way, their contents will take second place to the form of their communication, and you will be free to talk about promises, rather than making them.

Self-help is an awkward concept. What it means most of the time is helping yourself to feel better about making the same mistakes all over again. At best, a little bit of hypnotism can be produced: you can think of yourself in a new way or follow a handful of rules, but knowledge which is communicated in this form rarely has causal powers. Though not unknown, the revelatory effect is really quite rare: when the French theologian Malebranche picked up one of the first popular self-help manuals in a Paris bookshop, the *Discourse on the Method* by Descartes, he was so excited he had to stop reading every few lines and do breathing exercises. So great, indeed, was the impact of this book that another of Descartes' students refused to believe the news of his master's death, insisting that if it had really occurred, it must have been due to some mistake on the philosopher's part.

Such situations today may be hard to imagine, but the modern self-help volumes continue to sell. What they can certainly help you do is to buy the next volume which becomes modish, or you can be helped to wish you were someone else, but the tenor of your life probably won't change. In fact, it might even make your life much more difficult. Men and women all over the world are currently experiencing such difficulties after the publication of a little book called *The Rules*, with its thesis that the men women want should be treated like the men women don't want.

This is well and good, but the real problems are caused not by the fact that some women follow 'the rules' but rather because thousands of men are now convinced that women are following them who might not even have read the book. Uninterested women are assumed to be interested because they aren't showing too much interest, creating the comedy in which once again men think they have an idea what's on a woman's mind. Self-help thus contains the recipe for the perplexities and misfortune that envelop human nature, and shows how the only real rules are those that make us believe that someone else is following them. Just as beds do not come with instructions for how to sleep in them, lovers don't come with compendiums on how to calculate which set of rules they're following. The next best thing, of course, is to tell them, which is perhaps one of the reasons why a man might demand a promise from a woman about the future, which is the same thing as giving her a rule to live by. It is likewise impressive how manuals for the use of electronic equipment are always more complicated than self-help books. Unless their readerships are profoundly different, this means that a human is somehow considered simpler than a stereo, and easier to maintain.

What these volumes do show with such clarity is how, when men and women meet, it is not just a question of making a promise to a partner, but of demanding one. Women are told to obtain promises from men, and if they are also instructed to make them, it is not to the man but to themselves. This is a peculiar symmetry, and to explain it one could project the volume *Why do Women Make More Promises to Themselves Than to Men?* Although there are some reasons to believe that, self-help or no self-help, women often do make such silent vows, it is also a fact that it is men rather than women who most frequently ask their partners to promise something. One might assume that this is a sort of covert operation, to switch guilt to the side of the woman: if anything goes wrong, it's her that's made the promise, not him, as if his own doubts can be covered over by the apparent resolution of the partner. The bond of her promise thus works to obscure its foundation in the thought, 'She's not the one,' the man's perpetual uncertainty that he has found what he was looking for.

This might sometimes be the case, but it still leaves the question of why a man has so many doubts in the first place. The enthusiasm which often marks his first infatuations conceals sentiments which are hardly those of confederacy, and we shall see later on why this might be so. Although the encounter with another live human being will obviously introduce questions of their otherness and the ways in which they are different, it would be a mistake to assume that this supplies an explanation for the introduction of promises. One might suppose that this ignorance of the other person puts the future of a relationship in question, but this future may be determined before the other person has even been met.

Many people only enter into new relationships so that they can play out some little tragedy one more time with a new partner. Where it has been argued that it is a blindness about the future that requires the promiser to predict it boldly, one might add that this is often not a blindness about the future but a blindness about the past, and the way in which some pattern from childhood, for example, operates outside the scope of our conscious knowledge and obliges us to repeat things. A woman whose love life had no other vicissitude than the doubling of her partner compared herself unfavourably with her female friends: why could they settle for one man when she always had to have two? Finding Mr Right might be hard enough, she acknowledged, but aspiring to find two of them was folly, and hence she was left to bestow her favours on a selection of men whose taste and temper were adverse to her own. Yet the invariance of her design had its roots not in the failure to find one man but rather in the fact that one man, in the past, had been chosen. The memories of her childhood converged on a scene in which she is shopping with her father and the time has come to choose between two dresses: the father says 'You will have both' and it is this magnanimous gesture which came to provide a formula for her relation with the opposite sex. The uncertain future of these men was thus already inscribed in a commitment from the past.

Does all this mean that promising at the very start of a relationship is the sign that its ending is in sight? John Donne wrote, 'I am two fooles, I know, For loving, and for saying so.' Although one might choose to interpret this as a comment on the inability of language to express one's real feelings about love, it also suggests how saying that one loves may be fundamentally different from loving. The moment things pass to the level of the spoken word, things change: a certain limit has been crossed, and nothing can reverse this. Words cannot be taken back, and, crucially, they carry resonances and connotations picked up by the listener but unknown to the speaker.

When Katharine Hepburn's mother listened to the sermon of her father-in-law on the 'Giant Selfishness' of mankind, she was sure that his words were directed to her. When she confronted him angrily afterwards, he informed her that the sermon had in fact been written twenty years previously with a particular woman in mind: after the service, the latter had approached the Reverend to congratulate him on his speech, adding that it would do another woman in the congregation a lot of good. Such shifts of reference are introduced by writing as well as speaking: when Byron's 'Childe Harold' appeared, Lady Falkland was convinced that certain key passages referred to her, and this sort of skewed recognition is the source of much comedy. Balzac once said that his readers' efforts to identify the models of his fictional creations had taught him many domestic secrets of which he would otherwise have remained ignorant. Language makes us think that we are included, at some level, whether we like it or not, and it might be argued that the efficacy of the church sermon relies entirely on this principle.

And beyond the many possibilities introduced by speaking, there is the further question of why it was necessary to speak in the first place. When someone tells you something, it is one thing to meditate on the content of their message and another to wonder at why they actually told you when they did. When Joseph told his family the dream in which he and his brethren were all binding sheaves in a field, no one could get too upset, but when he added that his sheaf stood the tallest and that all the others bowed down to it he was taking risks. Telling them the second dream in which the sun, moon and stars repeated the same gesture of submission was really the nail in the coffin, and it is difficult to suppose that he didn't have the idea somewhere that all these exaggerated motifs of dominion would produce less an admiration of his candour than a counterattack. And likewise, telling your partner of an infidelity may seem like an act of compassionate honesty at one moment, and of pure malice at another. As Reik said, it is not silence that is golden, but tact: which means knowing when to speak and when to keep silent.

If loving and saying so thus have a relation which is not simply one of translation, Donne's line also indicates that foolishness is one of love's parts. It is often said that men in love are idiots, since their concerns seem to be contracted to one single thing, whereas women can maintain good sense.

But, dignified or not, a man who vows eternal love or demands eternal fidelity is also likely to talk silly. The baby talk between lovers is usually interpreted as just that: when Swift said things to Stella like 'Nite dealest' and 'Sawey dealest', it introduced the pantomime of infants. But, as everyone knows, infants don't talk like that. Baby talk is not the talk of babies but the speech of mothers *to* babies, which is not the same thing. According to one idea, baby talk expresses a state of security and comfort achieved by the lovers, a special language that is unique and personalised to their own particularity. The bedroom clock becomes 'Clocko', the duvet cover 'Mr Snug', words known and shared only by the couple. To talk like that would thus seem to involve treating one's partner as mother treats child, evoking the old idea that the real aim of love is to recreate in another person the mother's original delight in her baby. Just as she was delighted in you, you aim to make someone else delighted in yourself.

Many people, indeed, go through life with the concealed expectancy that the world will suddenly discover their hidden qualities. This may take the modest form of thinking that one's employers will recognise one's true abilities, or the more colourful conviction that one will be discovered as a star. But why is the baby talk so silly? It often takes the form of a personalised vocabulary for objects in the environment of the lovers. A woman whose husband was called Anthony called his penis 'Antonio', and this sort of charming investiture of the sex organs is very frequent. In some works of literature, the genitals even begin to speak, an idea that is no doubt behind the current vogue of talking animal films. If it might seem surprising to witness an animal endowed with speech, how much more surprising for the child to realise that the genitals do not obey its will, that there is a part of the body that seems to have a mind of its own. After this sort of shock, the next logical thing for genitals to do is to start talking. For some of the early fathers of the Church, male erection was a perpetual reminder of the fact that man had sinned and that he was now, sadly, no longer master of even his own body.

The silliness of baby talk is reflected in the silly things that lovers often give each other: furry animals and vegetables, useless objects of all sorts and enormous cards. The most favoured time of year to do this is also the date reserved for lovers, Valentine's Day. And what makes it the most important day in the calendar is not whether your partner sends you a gift or a card but whether he or she forgets to send you one. It shows that what is in question here is not just love but the *proof* of love, the articulation of love into signs. If it is indeed true that most Valentines are exchanged by couples already well ensconced in their relationships, the silly gift is less the sign that one is loved than the sign that one is *still* loved.

At the start of the film *Indecent Proposal*, Demi Moore asks her husband, 'Have I ever told you I love you? To his 'No', she replies 'I do', and to his 'Still?', she affirms 'Always'. This exchange, which is repeated throughout the film, has much charm but it does not quite ring true: if a man can say to a woman, 'Do you love me?', a woman is often more likely to say, 'Do you still love me?', and to the first question, reply with a request for information why. If Valentines are one way of saying 'Still', perhaps that is a reason for their different value for men and women, and how to say this 'Still' may be no simple matter. Many people complain that flowers and chocolates aren't quite right. They want to find something else, but are unsure, even uneasy, as to what that something is. Admittedly, some men show an inflexibility here. Lord Beaverbrook had the habit of sending his former mistresses £50 at Christmas and on his own birthday, thus sinking the illusion that he might have been thinking of anyone other than himself. The problem for most Valentines is that, on the contrary, they want the other party to know that they are indeed thinking of them, and not themselves. But the more you think of someone else, the more strange they become to you, the less like yourself, and the sentiment may skip from love to something else. Which is no doubt the reason why men and women sometimes choose to live together: to forget that, fundamentally, they are strangers.

So why the silliness at the time of remembering love? Like baby talk, it is less a decoration than an ingredient, showing us that at the centre of a love relation is something frighteningly silly, a little detail whose only meaning may be its place in the past. Some tiny sign that functions as a marker for a scene in childhood, for example, will set up the conditions necessary to fall in love. Stendhal compared the emergence of love with the production of a dazzling set of crystals from the humble origin of a bough thrown into the salt mine at Salzburg: without this initial element, the crystals which formed around it could not have appeared. And this is exactly what becomes clear at Valentine's Day. You can give flowers or books, objects with a symbolic meaning, but you could choose instead to give a fluffy bear with 'I love you' inscribed on it. A huge industry exists which has as its sole purpose the manufacture of such inane, meaningless objects and one may wonder whether the owners of the factories which produce them sometimes have thoughts about the meaning of life. Perhaps they spend their time reading Sartre, but the meaninglessness of their industry cannot, of course, be entirely without meaning. The popularity of such gifts at Valentine's Day is testimony to the way in which love always finds its soil in just this dimension of the ineffable, the stupid, the contingent. A lover's gift can thus have at least two forms: that of the crystal itself, the beautiful, captivating object, or something that represents the bough, a meaningless, stupid one. The countless fluffy animals and vegetables which change hands on Valentine's Day are really telling us something significant about love, even if we are only confronted with the powers of the tiny, meaningless detail when love twists on occasion into hate. The socks which were once looked on tenderly become terrible reminders of the man's unhealthy feet, his discarded shoes the index of a careless attitude and ultimate strangeness.

When André Breton and his friend, the cultural critic Roger Caillois, parted company, it was on exactly this question of the qualities of the detail. The Surrealist was fascinated by the mysterious energies of the jumping bean, while his friend insisted that they jump because of the presence not of some sort of marvellous property but rather of a worm or small insect inside them. It was a choice between the crystal and the bough, the brilliant quality or the contingent, unseemly detail. And one of the things that a psychoanalysis does is to perform a dissection of the jumping bean: to demonstrate that the container is, in one sense, empty, and in another sense the place where a little object has been lodged. When Alec and Laura first meet in the film *Brief Encounter*, their dialogue centres around the extraction of a little piece of grit which has become lodged in Laura's eye. It is from this initial, tiny detail that their romance burgeons, to the point at which he can say to her, 'I love you with all my heart and soul.'

If the piece of grit is at the base of the crystal, there is the further question of the process of transformation involved: how does the one produce the other? In *Brief Encounter*, it is no accident that Alec tells Laura about his vocation for preventive medicine, which focuses on a fibrosis of the lungs due to inhalation of particles of dust. The little detail thus matters so much as it strikes a chord with his phantasy, 'to extract a tiny object from a woman's body'. If love involves both a bough and a crystal, a romance and a piece of grit, this principle which transforms the one into the other is crucial, and it will have a different formula for each man and each woman.

❦

Choosing the crystal or the fluffy bear is an important decision, and perhaps the irresolution, or even anxiety, that becomes magnified as Valentine's Day approaches is the cover for another question: do we worry about the choice of present instead of worrying about the choice of partner, a worry which is left for all those days in between one Valentine's Day and another. And isn't it this that gives us a clue as to one striking feature of Valentine's cards – their anonymity. When couples lose the spark and have no horizon except routine, civilisation offers them techniques to turn each other, for a moment, into strangers: a new sexual position, a new costume for the bedroom, anything, that is, which rotates what you know into what you think you don't know. To refind your partner, you have to lose them first (which for some may take the form of having an affair). When the Valentine arrives with its 'x' in the place of a name, a stranger is made present, even if beyond it lies only the tedium of the spouse. Perhaps this is why most Valentines are exchanged between couples whose relation is already grounded, rather than between genuinely unknown lovers at a distance.

Some of the cards exchanged have another peculiarity. Besides their anonymity, they may be quite enormous, a feature which is not shared by the cards sent on birthdays or at

Christmas. Perhaps the most obvious point to be made about enormous cards is that they must be very difficult to hide. Imagine rewriting the classic scenes in literature and film where a lover swiftly conceals their love letter when another party enters the room. With today's gigantic cards, these scenes would become farce, even given the almost infinite recesses of eighteenth-century clothing. Such cards are tokens, then, that can't be hidden, that signal continuously the affection of the lover, but which, given their magnitude, cannot be filed after the date. In contrast to more conventional missives, their fate may well be the dustbin. The link between gigantic cards and the other object that is given the most on Valentine's Day, the flower, can hardly be accidental. The symbolic nature of this gift, the different significations linked to the different colour and variety of species chosen, can never hide the most obvious thing about them: they die quickly. This makes flowers the ideal lover's gift, as the fate of the flower reflects the most common issue of love: it ends.

Which brings us back to the question of promises, and of their classification in the list of the lover's baggage: do they belong with the flowers, with the dumb objects or with the crystals? In a sense, we ought to be getting worried already. Flowers don't last too long, dumb objects highlight the ineffable core of the passion of love which has little to do with the real partner, and crystals simply dazzle by obscuring the causes to which they owe their existence. This doesn't give promises much of a future.

It is this future which can end a sexual relation even before it starts. It is not uncommon for a woman to suddenly lose interest in the sexual act when she becomes aware, during foreplay perhaps, of some apparently unseemly aspect of her own person. A stain on one of her garments or a particular odour can kill the excitement, but this may be completely unknown to the man: all he sees is his partner's abrupt loss of arousal. This curious phenomenon hinges on the relation of time. The woman's arousal is dampened because she imagines the man's disgust with the aspect in question, an anticipation which supposes that the woman, at an unconscious level, has identified herself with the male partner. Hence the way in which a woman in love often seems more preoccupied with her own body than with that of the man. Where he will presumably feel disgust, so does she. She desires, then, from his place. And love can be curbed in a similar way. In Madame de Lafayette's novel *The Princess de Clèves*, a husband says to his wife, 'I have never been able to make you love me, and now I see that you are afraid of loving somebody else.' Although this fear may seem to herald the beginning of a real romance, it is by no means so certain: it may, on the contrary, mean that the man is avoided at all costs. And whereas a woman may avoid entering into any kind of relationship with a man because she is afraid of loving him, it is almost unheard of for a man to avoid a woman for the same reason. What a man may do is to become terrified of a sexual encounter with a woman, but he will not be terrified of loving her. Why is this?

The obvious answer lies in the fact that a woman may identify falling in love and giving herself completely. This is so dangerous because to give oneself completely means that one can be rejected completely. The whole of one's being is at stake, and hence the way in which, at the end of a love relation, a woman may feel like a different person. The old one, rejected, has been lost. This might help to explain, in turn, why it is the men who make promises: if a man is not afraid of loving, he can say all the things that he thinks lovers ought to be saying. A woman, on the contrary, if she is afraid of giving herself, may choose to be more silent.

The irony here is that this fear of falling in love conceals a form of love itself. In *Jamaica Inn*, Daphne du Maurier's heroine reasons to herself that the man she has recently met has few positive qualities: not only is he lacking in tenderness, he is also cruel and uncouth, as well as being a liar and a thief. And yet nonetheless, 'she knew she could love him'. This 'could' is in fact the sign that her passion has been set, showing the way in which a woman's love may begin with the thought 'I could love him' or 'I'm afraid of loving him', whereas the man's begins more probably when he says 'I love her'. And it shows, as a consequence, how leaving a man might be the best way of belonging to him.

This gives us a clue to the promises a woman might make at the start of a love relation, promises which are much less obvious than those of the man. She may make a promise not to her lover but *to herself*. For example, exactly the promise that she will never love some man. This produces a peculiar symmetry. If a man's promises of love are the sign that he is unsure of the future and are hardly propitious, a woman's promises *not* to love may sometimes be a much more powerful expression of love itself. Perhaps it would be more correct to call these resolutions instead of promises, since a promise is spoken aloud, while a resolution can be silent. The popular image of women speaking all the time has to be adjusted, and we can remember that Greek goddesses such as Aphrodite were celebrated not just for their tempers but for their silence. It may be true that when Charles I went off to seize the leading members of the Opposition, his Queen, unable to retain the information, babbled the secret to Lady Carlisle, but beyond the most dangerous gossip there is always something which a woman remains silent about.

Likewise, the idea that men remain reserved when it comes to speaking about what matters to them whereas women speak with ease and fluency about the most intimate things is seriously open to question. On an immediate level, this may seem persuasive as an observation. Women talk about the big things – emotions, pain, desire – whereas men's conversation is contracted to three concerns:

What they had to drink
How much of it they drank
What they did when they drank it.

Just as they had compared how far they could piss as boys, now they compare how much they have drunk as men. This might explain why the men in soaps are so appealing: although the action of the most popular series takes place in and around a place of drinking, the men actually talk about their worries, their joys and their despairs rather than discussing their relations to liquids. If this rings false for a man in the company of other men, it is certain that the man of today may try to say something, even everything, to his spouse. The topics of speech seem wondrously enlarged compared to those of the past. Where even the great sexologist Havelock Ellis, a man committed to the mysteries of the organism, was forced to receive his information by letter, being too timid to edge his subjects into conversation, these same matters may be the object of the compulsive candour of today's man. And in contrast to the disappearing man of the last centuries, always on the point of departure, the drama of the contemporary is exactly the opposite: he doesn't disappear enough. Where the old male heroes were always going off to war or to some adventure, many of the heart-throbs of today stay at home and talk meaningfully. And rather than saying too little, they say, on occasion, too much, even when it comes to love.

But speaking for the sexes does reveal its asymmetries. Linguists tell us that a man's speech involves a contest, while a woman's is about consensus. Men disagree with or ignore each other's utterances, while women acknowledge or build on them. Where a woman will use questions to continue a conversation, a man will interpret these as simple requests for information. Two men will often walk down a street and continue a conversation without looking at each other, but for two women this is practically impossible. And, of special importance, if a man may find it important to feel loved, a woman may want to be told, and this is where all the interesting problems about speaking start. Why should the value of speech be different for many men and women here? We find a clue in a novel which is famous for having one word missing: Daphne du Maurier's *Rebecca*. This carefully constructed romance became the centre of a literary puzzle: Why did Daphne fail to give a name to the main character in her book, the narrator?

She claimed that she just couldn't think of one, but when Hitchcock, in his scripts for the screen version, filled in her identity as 'Daphne de Winter', his addition missed the crucial point. *Rebecca* is the story of a young lady who meets, marries and then moves in with Mr de Winter, a man haunted by the presence of his dead wife, the Rebecca of the title. As the young lady narrates her story, we learn of her obsession with this first wife, and much of the storytelling centres on the difficulties for her of going into the place of this other woman. Whereas Rebecca was assertive, bold and vigorous, the narrator is timid, shy and incapable, until the one moment in the text when her husband reveals to her that he had never loved Rebecca and that he had even gone so far as to murder her. From now on, the narrator has found her wits and proves autonomous and resourceful, showing how *Rebecca* is the narrative of a woman finding her identity in relation to the place of another woman. If her own feminine identity is a question mark, it is through the lethal image of the first wife and her husband's relation to her that she finally comes to take on a place in the world she has entered. Du Maurier's failure to name the narrator is thus no accident: the empty place of the name is the place of the question mark of identity, and Susan Hill, in her sequel to the book, remains true to du Maurier in her choice of title: *Mrs de Winter*, once again suggesting that the identity of the heroine is always constructed through the identity of others. It can take the form of the identity of the dead wife or, in the sequel, that of the wife of the husband.

In each case, the formula is something like: another woman was there first. And the place of the other woman takes on its value in being the focus of a man's desire: what did he desire in her and what does he desire in me? How else could one explain the deluge of letters and parcels that Tom Hanks received in *Sleepless in Seattle*? After his son phones a radio show to complain of his father's loneliness, the latter talks about the dead wife he loved so much, her beauty and the way they had first touched hands. Meg Ryan is understandably reduced to tears, as are thousands of women across America, each one dreaming of occupying the place of this absent woman in the man's love. It is thus not Tom Hanks himself who is so interesting, but the relation between him and the dead wife: like Rebecca, she embodies the place of the woman loved by a man. When Meg Ryan finally ends her quest and meets the man of her yearning, she places her hand on his in exactly the way in which he had described the gesture of the dead woman. She may have wished to be loved for herself, but the framework which captures her is based on the place of another woman.

This priority suggests a neat solution to one of the great controversies of biblical scholarship: if Eve was the original woman, how can one account for the assorted references to

Lilith, who seems to have been there first? The logic of *Rebecca* shows that there will always be someone prior to Eve: to be the first, there has to be one before. Identity is elaborated in relation to the shadow of another woman and, crucially, there is the question of a man's relation to the one who was there first. Eve might have had some worries about the business with the apple, but it is sure that she would have been equally vexed with thoughts of Adam's relation to Lilith. Perhaps she imagined tender scenes of dialogue between them, and if she did, the serpent would certainly have known what to say to produce a little transgression, evoking softly some detail of Lilith's body or her spirited nature. This indicates a first response to the question of the different value of telling for the sexes. If identity is a question mark, to be loved 'as someone' can supply a measure of being.

Being told why one is loved may never be satisfactory, but it can still supply an identity, through charting the place a woman occupies for someone else, what they mean for them. Hence the way in which a woman, after a disappointment in love, may seem to lose her 'old self' and literally become 'a new person', changing haircut, clothes and image. That this is not a finite process is seen in the fact that women who become mothers have more changes of hairstyle in the year following giving birth than at any other time in their lives. Becoming a mother might seem to promise a new identity, but, to the delight of professional hairdressers, this identity is hardly a fixed one; and hence the quest for a new image to step into.

It is in fact into the image of Rebecca that the heroine steps quite literally in du Maurier's book. Goaded on by the sly housekeeper Mrs Danvers, she chooses as her ballgown a dress depicted in one of the portraits at Manderley. As she stands at the top of the stairs ready to make her appearance, the horrified looks of the early guests swiftly allow her to understand what has happened: she has chosen the same dress as Rebecca had worn at the last party there before her death. If Rebecca had stepped into the dress of the woman in the portrait, the nameless heroine now steps into the place of Rebecca. Stepping into her dress is, for her, to step into her image. The structure here was grasped quickly by the *News of the World* after the actor Hugh Grant was apprehended in a car with Divine Brown, engaged in a sexual act. What initially mystified the public was how the partner of the beautiful and glamorous Elizabeth Hurley could do something so apparently lacking in both beauty and glamour. Why would the man who had everything act like a man without means? Grant's relation with Hurley was first brought to the public eye when Hurley wore an amazing Versace dress at a film première. The dress, stuck together niftily with safety pins, caused a sensation. Now, after the arrest of Grant and general publicity over the escapade, the *News of the World* carried on its front page a photo of Divine Brown in the same Versace dress, with the headline 'It's that tart in that dress'. If the dress was at first the defining feature of Hurley, it was now shifted to Brown, the image into which each woman stepped, exactly like the dress in *Rebecca*.

The newspaper's impolite act was in this displacement, suggesting as it did that one woman could step into the place of another in the love life of a man, provided that the frame stayed the same. Identity was thus something like a gown to be stepped into, rather than any intrinsic natural property. It implied that, for the man, the dress was the key feature, and whoever stepped into it suddenly became attractive. Which is what usually happens with men. The mention of one little detail can arouse desire instantly, be it a feature of a dress or something overheard: the safety pin or the fact that the woman in question is desired by another man.

One should not forget, however, that Divine was *not* wearing that dress until that newspaper gave it to her. Whether the two women had something else in common is a matter known only to the parties concerned, but it is just as likely that what mattered for the actor was their difference, demonstrating the Freudian mechanism by which an idealised woman is loved but not desired and a degraded woman is desired but not loved. Since the woman is linked by a chain of associations to the mother, and since it is unbearable to contaminate the mother's image with sexuality, the ideal and the sexual are neatly split into two. Love and sexual desire thus separate, and each current takes its own object, the ideal lady and the degraded one. But what would have happened if the *News of the World*'s conceit had been no fiction, and the two women had not only worn the same dress but had actually met each other wearing it?

It is the nightmare of many women not to step into the other woman's dress but to meet her at a party when they are both wearing it. The narrator of *Rebecca* would meet her double only in the horrified gaze of husband and guests, but another Rebecca would encounter her in flesh and blood, detail for detail. After her husband had given both Rebecca West and his mistress the same expensive handbag, the two women would meet face to face, each with their new gift. But rather than snubbing her rival, Rebecca welcomed the confused ballet teacher with her exclamation, 'Oh how lovely! We've both got one.' The pronoun was particularly well chosen, as it evoked both the handbag and the husband, although the sentence in its entirety expressed exactly the opposite of what mattered for the two women. Having the same bag is the stamp not of difference but of sameness, more importantly, sameness in the eyes of a man, a quality at odds with the requirement for a woman that she be different. This is the reason for the worldwide success of the Spice Girls. These talented singers belong to the same set – the set 'Spice' – but the crucial thing about them is that they are all different. Whereas a man may wish to be appreciated as 'a man', a woman may aim to be admired not only as a member of her own sex but as 'herself'. The Spice Girls are all members of a group, but they are just not the same: they are all Spice, but there is Baby Spice, Posh Spice, Scary Spice . . . Where other groups dress up in the same clothes and have their hair arranged in the same way, each of these women is different from the others, yet they nonetheless share an identity. They belong and don't belong at the same time. The failure to respect this condition is what got Falstaff into so much trouble in *The Merry Wives of Windsor*. Mistress Page and Mistress Ford might both belong to the set 'Merry Wives', but when Falstaff sends them an identical love letter, the two women give him hell to pay. Making two women the same, he was punished for his ignorance of the most basic requirement: that each one be different. And crucially, that each one can compare herself trait by trait with the other woman, where each comparison produces one asymmetry: 'She's got a lovely smile, but my eyes are more beautiful; she's got finer hair, but my neck is more exquisite . . .'

A book like *Rebecca* is indeed a book about comparisons: not only does the narrator continually compare herself with her husband's dead wife, she imagines that he is doing the same thing too. 'Whenever you touched me,' she says to him, 'I thought you were comparing me to Rebecca. Whenever you spoke to me or looked at me, walked with me in the garden, sat down to dinner, I felt you were saying to yourself, "This I did with Rebecca, and this, and this."'

One might be tempted to explain this feature of a continued comparison by evoking the figure of the mother: what matters to a daughter will be the ways in which she is different from her parent. And indeed, many psychoanalytic writers identify the problem in daughter–mother relations as a kind of push towards similarity combined with a pull towards difference: she must become *like* her mother, yet never *become* her. To be like her would put the daughter in the place of the one who receives the father's desire, and yet, if this desire is important for her, that makes the mother her rival, the one who must be disposed of. It is therefore the same dynamic that pushes her towards the mother that will pull her away.

But does this really explain the magnification in *Rebecca* of the woman who was there first? The narrator seems dwarfed by another woman, the dead wife, yet in Daphne du Maurier's autobiography there are few references to her own mother. In her novel, there is the massive shadow of another woman, but in her story of her life, there is no comparable female presence. It might be argued here that since the mother failed to provide any image of femininity for her daughter, the latter would be led to idealise the images of other women. Hence the dominant presence of Rebecca. But one could object that it is not simply a question of the mother's failure, but of the daughter's making the mother fail: she has been written out of the story, in the same way that when a text is being censored the most important part will be left out. Thus, the rivalry with the mother serves to remove her.

This reminds one of the great dispute about the role of Dora's mother. In Freud's celebrated and forever maligned case history, we hear hardly anything about the mother, suggesting to many critics that she must therefore have a special importance. While it is quite correct to formulate arguments from omissions, to ask why something is missing and not simply why something is there, the Dora case and the du Maurier structure in fact suggest something slightly different. As the psychoanalyst Geneviève Morel has pointed out, in Freud's great case histories the mother is devalued in a very precise way: she is overlooked by the father in favour of someone else. Thus Dora's father has an affair with Mrs K, and in the case of the Rat Man the patient's father marries a woman for her money, when his real interest is with a woman from his past. The recipe for problems is when the father fails to give the mother a certain place in the family, the place of the cause of his own desire. This may seem like an obvious point, but the key is to distinguish love and desire here. The problem would be when the husband loves the wife too much, rather than situating her as the cause of his desire. And if the wife no longer functions to cause the desire of the man, it is not, perhaps, to her that the daughter will turn, a conclusion which seems to support the other explanation for the magnification of the woman in *Rebecca*. Daphne's own mother was certainly a woman bypassed by her father in the continuing cycle of his affairs. This does not rule out the cases in which the father does genuinely desire the mother, and the logic here has to be refined. Perhaps a folk tale can sharpen the form of some of these problems.

A queen dies, and the king decides that he can only marry someone equally fair. But who could possibly be as fair as the dead wife? Only one person: the daughter. In response to this understanding, the daughter not only exiles herself, she also sacrifices her hands. This strange but amazingly common motif is explained by critics in different ways, either as a means of rendering the daughter unfit for marriage with the king by becoming unlike her mother (who had hands) or due to the fact that the hands were particularly attractive to the father. She thus gives him the most beautiful part of herself, and frequently she will find a man (another king) who loves her (despite her lack of hands). Glossy magazines are forever publishing lists of things that matter to a woman, and although the motif of no hands does not tend to feature in such catalogues, we could follow their example and extract from the folk tale a set of central concerns a daughter may have in relation to her parents:

the death of the mother and the question of taking her place
the question of comparison, of being as fair as someone else
the giving up of a part of the body
being loved despite, or because of, this lack
the question of making oneself unlike the mother
the idea of an exile, a solitude linked to the father's love.

The story provides a sort of parallel myth to that of Oedipus, and just as Oedipus is the story of a man with a foot problem (Oedipus = swollen foot), this is the story of a woman with a hand problem. In many versions, the daughter has been brought up away from the father's sight. Her sudden appearance before the king in complete adult beauty and resemblance to the mother captivates him, to generate the common romance motif of the father's being reminded of his dead wife by the image of the daughter. If this story is a feminine one, there is still, in this latter conceit, a perfect encapsulation of the male oedipal structure: a man falls in love with a woman due to her 'identity' with a mother. Women, however, often express their rage at being compared to their mothers. If a man wants to find a woman to mother him, he often makes a big mistake in *telling* her that she's like a mother. What ushers in the romance, in being articulated, can end it.

These fairy stories are about the tensions unleashed when a woman goes into the place of the mother, and in general, if a woman goes into the place of another woman *consciously*, it will be someone else, a woman somehow separated from the mother. Hence the way in which many girls copy their mothers until, at adolescence, they reject them with the greatest determination, setting up the image of another woman as ideal. And, as is well known, it is often at pregnancy that the image of the mother returns to haunt them with a vengeance.

This problematic of substitution may be central to the psychic life of a woman and yet, as we shall see, it is not really a question of a daughter substituting herself for her mother. Substituting and being different from are not the same thing, and it is interesting to note how in *Rebecca*, although for one woman it seems to be a question of taking the place of someone else, for another there can never be any question of this. The figure of the housekeeper Mrs Danvers is the embodiment of this principle, 'One woman can never be substituted for another.' Even after her beloved Rebecca has died, she remains faithful to the image of the wife, as if her place can never be dislodged.

This can give us a clue to a problem noted by the psychoanalyst Helene Deutsch. Given the fact that our society has been patriarchal for a long time and that women have been in the place of objects exchanged by men, why is it, she asked, that so many women have the fantasy of being sold into the slave trade, not by a ruthless man but by a woman? Why is it the woman here who is the agent of the betrayal? Is the woman linked to the mother, ruthless and evil because she has in fact failed to stand up to the male discourse and assert the independence of her sex? Or is it due to the callousness of the mother that she is allowed to enter the circuit of exchange itself in the first place? The woman wants her out of the house, and so sends her packing to the circuit of men. But the image of Mrs Danvers nuances this idea: it serves to maintain a separation between two registers, one in which women are exchanged and one in which they are not. De Winter's dead wife Rebecca stays out of the circuit, and, for Mrs Danvers, can never find a substitute. If any other woman could be substituted for the new wife, no other woman can be exchanged for the old one. This does not mean that Mrs Danvers herself represents the mother, but rather that her presence shows the split between the two registers, one which follows the law of exchange and one which doesn't. In the fantasy discussed by Helene Deutsch, the female slave trader retains a consistency, an evil stability that contrasts with the register of substitution into which she sends the women, suggesting that female sexuality may be concerned simultaneously with *both* exchange and the refusal of exchange. Which gives us a clue to understanding the strange figure of Mrs Danvers: although one may assume hastily that she must be some kind of 'bad mother', the most obvious and at the same time the most hidden feature of du Maurier's character is that, in her passion for the lost woman of the past, Mrs Danvers is in precisely the place of a daughter. Although a woman may transfer her affections to a man, there is still one solid, painful and irreversible commitment that cannot be forgotten, even if a woman may spend her entire life trying to do so. In her refusal to accept any substitute, it is this terrible commitment to the mother that Mrs Danvers embodies.

Rebecca may be a book about the shadow of another woman, but it is also a book about *people not saying things*. As the narrator uncovers more facts about the suspicious past of her husband, she systematically fails to voice them, just as her husband, Mr de Winter, continually fails to talk about what really happened to his first wife. It is thus a narrative about people not telling each other things. Susan Hill's sequel continues this thread: as the heroine becomes involved in an unsavoury blackmail plot, there is no one, she thinks, she can tell. Hill's narrator remains just as silent about the awful visit of Mrs Danvers as du Maurier's does about the appearance of Rebecca's cousin, Mr Favell. But why doesn't she just tell her husband?

The enigma of this silence is exactly what led Lewis Carroll to despair when he was reading *Much Ado About Nothing*: as Claudio rejects Hero on her wedding day for an infidelity of which she is innocent, Carroll simply couldn't understand why she didn't just say that she had not been sleeping in her room on the night in question. What he ignored was the possibility that in not saying something, more is at stake than simple information. People don't pass through their lives exchanging facts, since sexuality gets in the way, and sexuality has a special link with secrets and with not saying things. In *An Affair to Remember*, Cary Grant and Deborah Kerr arrange a date at the top of the Empire State Building six months in advance, but an accident on her way to the crucial rendezvous prevents her from showing up. As the story continues, with each character going about their separate lives, the big question is: Why doesn't she just tell him why she wasn't there? Why generate so much suffering, suspicion and misunderstanding when all it would have taken was a phone call?

One could project a BT advert with Bob Hoskins desperately trying to convince her to pick up the phone, but his success would only transport fiction into pure fantasy. She says later on in the film that she wanted to be able to walk again before contacting him, but her silence has a more opaque quality. A secret, whether it is trivial or not, may take on a sexual value for the sole reason of its not being communicated. In not being said, it evokes the register of the forbidden, of something not passed into the circuit of speech. The heroine of *Rebecca* and *Mrs de Winter* is haunted by the question 'Is my husband a murderer?', but in both books she is hampered from bringing such thoughts to the level of speech. This barrier is linked, perhaps, to the question of what it means to be a woman which echoes throughout du Maurier's book. The psychoanalyst Karen Horney once detailed her fantasy about the perfect male partner: he would be a man who anticipated her to such an extent that she would never have to ask for anything. She would thus be in the position of a woman who does not speak, but also in the position of a woman who does not desire. If the man has everything ready for her whenever necessary, her desire will be satisfied before it even has time to articulate itself. And in this fantasy, the desire is shifted over to the side of the man: all the activity seems to be on his side, as he devotes his existence to understanding his lover.

The question of her identity is thus broached through someone else, as in *Rebecca*, but with a rather different consequence. Rather than generating in her any kind of autonomy, placing desire on the side of the man puts her in the position of the woman in her other major fantasy scenario: someone who bows down to a great and powerful male figure. The two scenarios thus follow the same initial logic, and the lack of speaking means, in this case, the failure to assume a desire. It is therefore no accident that the moment the narrator begins to speak in *Rebecca* is also the moment at which she seizes her wits, the moment at which she becomes identical, literally, with a desire, and starts to do things . . .

If *Rebecca* focuses to such an extent on the problem of speaking, we are led back to the motif of speaking itself and its value. Why should the motif of something not being said remain so captivating? In folklore and fairy tales, daughters don't speak in two important ways: they either just don't say what's on their mind or they are blocked from speaking by another woman, often the mother, mother-in-law or stepmother. This is interesting, and poses the question of the relation between these two possibilities. If women have had many problems in speaking due to the efforts of a patriarchal society to silence them, why is the agency which obstructs them in these stories embodied by a woman? To say that fairy tales are a male invention is the same thing as saying that one has never listened to any. Although they have been compiled and revised by men, fairy tales privilege the themes closest to a woman: sisterhood, the relations with the mother and her representatives, childbirth and the conflicts between women. This might seem to imply that it is the shadow of the mother which keeps the daughter silent. In one popular tale, a prince out riding finds a lifeless maiden lying in a coffin. She is revived and the pair of them marry and have children. Yet the prince's devotion to the bride makes his mother rather upset. She cuts off the heads of their children and puts them onto the new queen's bed. When the husband sees this and hears the mother's accusations, he banishes his wife, after having her hands cut off. And yet during all this commotion, the innocent woman remains silent. Eventually, she regains her hands and the children are brought to life, she gets a castle, meets her husband again and breaks her silence. The mother is then put into a barrel of pitch and thrown into the sea.

This story is instructive, and yet isn't it just another male narrative: why else, after all, would there be the drama of the prince's mother getting all upset when her son's affections are redirected? But this is exactly one of the factors that makes it not a male narrative: it is the sensitivity to the mother's jealous attentions, and the fact of giving them a central, even an exaggerated place, which has a more feminine accent. We can first of all note that it is a woman who is behind another woman's silence, and secondly, that she can speak again once the missing parts of the body have been restored. The failure to speak in *Rebecca* could thus be explained in terms of the oppressive shadow of the other woman, the dead wife of Mr de Winter, with the nuance that desire and speaking seem closely linked. But why should the silence itself have such powerful effects? Why do readers remain so anxious that something ultimately be said, that a message, in the end, be delivered?

Many works of literature and cinema are concerned with exactly this problem, seen most clearly in those scenarios in which someone is desperate to deliver a message but everything around them contrives to block its receipt. In Zola's novel *Thérèse Raquin* an old woman learns that her beloved daughter-in-law and her new husband had been the murderers of her adored son. Helpless and unable to appeal for help due to a paralysis, she saves all her remaining energies for the Thursday night social gathering that has become a regular feature of family life. As she desperately moves her fingers, the company assumes she wants to join in their game of dominoes, and when she starts to trace letters on the tabletop, her gesture is interpreted as an approbation for the play of a double six. With the last of her strength she inscribes the names of the murderers and the word 'have', yet the excited guests finish her sentence for her with the phrase 'been very good to me'. Her desperate pleas are thus transformed into harmless informations and the guilty parties become more cherished by their company than condemned.

The scene is drawn out and painful, as it orchestrates almost in slow motion someone not being heard, having their message torn away from them and lost. And this from Zola, an author celebrated for his passion to speak the truth, to deliver a message to society. It might be argued here that the central narrative of Christianity is concerned with exactly this problem: someone has a message to deliver to mankind, but mankind does not always hear it properly. In this sense, the story of Christ is the story of someone who is trying to speak, to say something, and hence the ancient identification of the appearance of the Son with a kind of divine stammering. The same motif of desperate communication is common in science fiction narratives. Someone arrives from the future with a crucial life-saving message for mankind, but it is not heard. In *Terminator 2* and in Terry Gilliam's *12 Monkeys*, a character carries the message of the future destruction of mankind, yet the world's failure to believe means that they are, in both stories, interned. And this is of course what happens in real life: when someone is convinced that they have a message to deliver to mankind, the most common diagnosis is madness. This may be the case even when the message is in fact true. When the Hungarian physician Semmelweis insisted in a delusional way that strict hygienic standards had to be met when childbirth took place, although his behaviour was paranoiac, the idea of the delusion was quite correct. It was not the idea, however, which made him mad, but his certainty as to its truth.

Such narratives rely on our involvement in the pain of transmitting a message, and, if these stories end happily, it will be at the moment when the protagonist finally finds someone who will believe his story. Like the children's game of Chinese whispers, the message must go full circle, and the difference between this game and the many books and films which treat of the same theme gives us a clue to its power. As the message is whispered from one child to another, it becomes distorted, and the wonder is in comparing the initial sentence with the final product. If the game itself has a message, it is that language has a distorting effect, that what you begin with will not be what you end up with, and that when something is put into the circuit of speech, it won't come out the same as it went in. The message in Chinese whispers is always lost, whereas in the many cultural versions of the story of the man with the message, it usually tends to arrive. It is recognised, and the message of the end becomes that of the start. The reason why audiences become so involved in these narratives is the motor of the original children's game, the fact that in entering the world of language we have lost something: as we ask for something, we must use speech, but from the moment we use speech a whole set of other considerations come into play. What one had originally asked for becomes secondary, since what matters now is whether the other replies or not, whether they show a sign of love or not in their response. If someone keeps calling you up asking for things, it is clear that it is not the things that are important, but the asking.

Stockbrokers know that the insistent calls of many of their clients are not primarily directed to the acquisition of the latest market information, but represent the form of an unconditional demand, a priority given not to financial profit but to the greed of repetitive asking itself. The genre of comedy relies on this displacement: that when you ask for one thing, you get something else, be it the wrong person in your bed or a letter that was destined for someone else. The particularity of neurosis here is the abdication from the difficult task of trying to send a message oneself. In paranoia, the message can never be sent by someone else: it is the mission of the speaker to deliver it, but a neurotic, we could say, is someone who insists on sending messages through other people (or even, who desires through other people). When it arrives at its destination, someone else can be blamed for the distortion, and the sender can slip away in silence. When lovers whisper their promises late at night, perhaps the same set of concerns is involved: to transmit a message and to have the message received in all its intimacy. Just as the saviour from the future searches for someone to listen to his tale, so the promiser aims at finding someone who will hear him. Which throws things back from the particularity of the partner to that of the promiser: what matters is not the being of the beloved, but whether someone can be found to recognise the one who speaks, to guarantee to him that he's been heard, to find a real listener . . . in other words, to find someone who will do what language won't do.

Elaborating on these themes, Lacan turned to Molière's *The School for Wives*, a play which brings into focus the problems of sending a message and the sincerity of speech. Agnès is an apparently innocent and naive girl, brought up in a convent in accordance with the stifling pedagogy of Mr Arnolphe. This sorry figure intends to make her his conforming bride, until his plans are disrupted by a young beau, Horace, who has his own designs on the girl. It seems that *The School for Wives* is the story of a woman caught in between two men, but as Lacan reads it, it emerges more as the choice between two forms of speech, two discourses. On the one hand, the educative, supposedly unambiguous discourse of Arnolphe, and on the other the cunning and equivocal speech of Horace. Agnès' adventure is the journey into the world of speech, as the play shows her passage from the object of Arnolphe's pedagogy into a real speaking being, someone who can speak for herself rather than be spoken by a discourse imposed on her.

The question for commentators on the play has always been to determine whether this apparently naive young creature was really as naive as all that: in her eventual deceptions of her guardian, was there a malign and resolute will or simply the play of circumstance? Did she really mean to cause a lot of trouble or was that just the way things turned out? In other words, what the critics debate is Agnès' subjectivity, what is supposed to be 'really' there at the core of her actions. Lacan, however, had a different perspective: less the supposed subjectivity behind her speech than the fact that in speaking, her desire would always be out of reach, ungraspable, different from what she seems to demand at the manifest level. Thus, even when she tells Arnolphe the truth, something else is signified by her speech, whether she likes it or not. When Arnolphe tells her to rebuff the beau's approaches by throwing a stone down at him from her window, she does this, but omits to add that she had attached a message to it. The key point here is that her apparently wily actions can be understood as less the behaviour of Agnès than that of speech itself: whatever you say, because you are speaking, something else will be signified, something beyond the obvious message, just as there is more to the stone than the stone itself. It is not her intentions which make her a 'phony', as many critics have supposed, but the very fact of speaking, which makes of her, to use the description of Holly Golightly in *Breakfast at Tiffany's*, a 'real phony'. Which is very different from a phony phony.

Holly Golightly is an affected, distracted, unconventional and breezy woman who meets the serious, sincere and solid writer Paul Varjac. But, right from the start, we realise that it is he who sells his sexual services for money, while Holly implies them without committing herself. Behind Varjac's sincerities are the calculations of a kept man: when he speaks to the woman who pays his rent, for example, he conceals things with purpose, but Holly, on the contrary, lets speech itself make the promises she doesn't. She relies, unlike Varjac, on the fact that speaking always implies more than it says, a quality of language that eventually leads to her social downfall. Each week, she visits Sing Sing to chat with a mafia boss behind bars, returning to New York with a 'weather report' for his lawyer. All she tells him is 'It's snowing in Palermo' or 'There's a hurricane in Cuba', but, like the stone with its letter attached for Agnès, this empty message means more than it says, and it gets her into a lot of trouble. As her agent says, what makes her a real phony rather than a phony one is the fact that 'she believes all the nonsense that she believes'. Her affectations are real ones, in the sense that Holly is a mask, but behind this there are only other masks, whereas for Varjac there are the hidden conceits of his ambition. Where Varjac hesitates to admit to the symbols of his greed, Holly makes no effort to hide her wish for money or fame: if she is a genuine phony, he is therefore the phony one. Molière's Agnès and Holly, although separated by centuries, thus enjoy the solidarity supplied by speaking.

To these fictional creatures may be added another nonfictional one, a woman who nonetheless inhabited a world of the weavers of fiction. When the poet Heine entered a shop in the rue Choiseul, he fell in love instantly with the woman he was to marry and adore, Mathilde. Heine scholars have always been horrified at the presence of this woman, and she is described in the literature as 'shallow', 'empty-pated', 'heedless', 'extravagant', 'a bad housekeeper', 'a worse cook', 'frivolous', 'a minx' and 'the very antithesis of romance'. But, they all agree, she was a natural. This was a woman who had the power to persuade a troop of French soldiers to go looking for her lost parrot

Cocotte in the woods of the Pyrenees, and, on overhearing her husband's doctor tell him that he needed better attention, to wait for him in the passage outside and give him a black eye. She stayed with Heine for twenty years, and her fidelity was so powerful that she chose to die, twenty-seven years after his own death, on the very same day, surrounded by spaniels, canaries and parrots. While the words of the poet and his colleagues were forever being plumbed for hidden analogies and latent meanings, when Mathilde spoke everything just appeared to be there at the surface, to the horror of the poet's literary friends. Like Holly, her directness was disconcerting, and the fact that it seemed nothing was being hidden was a scandal. How, after all, can speech not have something to hide? Which brings us back to the question of what it means to tell the truth and what it means to 'tell' in the first place.

Two

At what moment can a human being truly be said to speak? Machines can be built which replicate sounds and even reproduce them at appropriate moments. But replication and simple articulation are not the same as speech. Something more is necessary, and many of the scholars who have turned their attention to this problem have agreed on what it is: lying. A child may learn that certain signs in his linguistic environment will produce certain effects: crying, for example, may result in feeding, even if hunger was not the original cause of the distress. The French writer Marcel Pagnol describes the painful spectacle of seeing his infant cousin utter formless gurgles, to which his aunt 'replied with real words to make us believe that he had said something intelligent'. The gurgles, taken up in the speech of the mother, now take on a meaning, but this meaning comes not from within but from without.

And as language is learnt, there is often the moment, as Lacan points out, when it appears to the child that the adults around him know his thoughts. They know his thoughts for the simple reason that his thoughts, being words, come from them. Born into a world of language, the thoughts are there before him. They are, in this sense, the property of others. It is only when it becomes possible to separate these thoughts from the parents that the key phase is reached, when the child, by withholding something, can demonstrate that he or she is separate from his or her words. Which is the first lie, the barrier between what one says and how one is different from one's words. In a similar way, the lie can take on the form of exploring the possibilities of speech to create what isn't there. Children often fabricate 'imaginary friends', a phenomenon which is sometimes explained in terms of the child's relation to the body image. But an imaginary friend is first and foremost the product of speech, a way of making something exist solely through words: it is through speaking that a new member of the family circle comes into being. The lie, the imaginary friend and the promise can thus form a series: all of them rely on the possibilities of speech, and all of them make something exist with nothing other than words.

If an imaginary friend can be made to exist with speech, could a wolf be materialized in the same way? In the famous story of the boy who cried 'Wolf!', the question of whether it was his first word or not remains unexplored. If it was, he begins speaking with an untruth, but he does so in the same way as every child who speaks. A child can say a particular word when it sees some animal, and even call the animal by the sound it is supposed to make: there's a moo or a mee-ow. But speaking involves more than the blind duplication of sounds: sounds have to be combined and separated, moved around and substituted for each other. Otherwise, there's no speech. That's why the child who says 'There's a moo' when it sees a cow cannot necessarily speak: speaking comes when it can say the same thing when it sees not a cow but a duck, showing how bits of language are being shifted around. Mothers are familiar with the time, around twenty months, when the child applies the same term to many different objects: everything becomes the 'moo', from the duck to the cow to the telephone. Perhaps the boy who cried 'Wolf!' was around this age, and the unfriendly response of his parents showed nothing but an ignorance of modern linguistics. He wasn't telling them that a wolf was there, just organising his world with language, learning to speak like all the other good boys on the block.

The classical interpretation of this story, however, is to see it as the tragic history of a thwarted demand for love. The boy is neglected by his parents and left to inhabit his own fantasy world. When he cries 'Wolf!', it is to excite the attention of his parents, when all other attempts to interest them have failed. Sadly, he is no longer given any credence by the time the real wolf shows up, and he is swallowed, perhaps as a lesson to all of those children who raise the alarm in false circumstances. If the child's 'Wolf!' may be understood as his first real speech, what about trying to understand the motives of the listeners, the adults around him? Would the repetition of an untruth be so likely to make the listeners close their ears? The Scottish philosopher Hume was surely wrong to say that a person who breaks a promise is never trusted again. In fact, it is exactly this quality which may be the decisive feature in rendering someone irresistible. If a man forever fails to turn up where he is expected or obviously continues to see several women at once, the absence of any exclusivity may be just what is necessary to make a woman aim at being the exception, at being different from all the others he has deceived. Once a man is found who maintains a series of women through his broken promises, there might be the desire to belong to the series in a special way, as the one who really counts, to whom the promise will not lie. Love does not necessarily end when a lie of the partner is revealed, and may come to inhabit precisely that space.

In the very first scene of the 1950s film *The Blob*, Steve McQueen is on a date with a girlfriend at a local beauty spot. As a shooting star whistles over them, she is surprised at his equanimity, and he responds by telling her that it is not an uncommon sight. Upon which the girl asks him angrily if he is so well informed due to his visits there with a medley of women. Being perhaps more instructed in celestial phenomena than in female ones, he says no, and it is only once this obvious lie has been uttered that the story of the blob from outer space can really get started. This unpleasant thing is never described in the film as 'the blob', but as 'something that keeps getting larger'. Rather than understanding this in the phallic sense, so that the more the young couple fail to make love, the bigger the blob gets, which would make of the film a fable of small town sexual repression, we might see it instead as a version of Pinocchio's nose which, as he utters falsehood, keeps getting larger. This would imply that if speaking involves a first lie, and if lying creates the blob, each speaker will have to deal with something that keeps getting bigger. And all this starts from the initial lie, which, although the girlfriend knows that it is a deception, allows her to stick with him throughout the film.

Men who are not true to their word may thus exert a certain fascination, but what about a woman who does not tell the truth? Some men seem to get worried when a woman *does* tell the truth too often, perhaps because they are quite happy to believe that she is hiding something. When Mme de Sommery's lover arrived at the wrong time, he was confronted with the scene of his mistress in the arms of another man. Bravely denying everything, she cried 'You don't love me any more: you'd rather believe your eyes than what I tell you!' This excellent story may serve as a starting point for the philosophers who study the problems of sense perception and knowledge, showing as it does a priority given to speech over what is seen, and the action of the heart in making one blind. In this example, the lover who arrived at the wrong time cried 'Wolf!', and, just like the unfortunate hero of that fable, he failed to obtain the acknowledgement he required. Even when the wolf was really there, the sanguine lady denied its presence, evoking love to make of herself the only lupine present. As she commands him to believe a word and not his eyes, the lady of the salon becomes the wolf in chic clothing, and her lover the victim of all the words of love which he had uttered without weighing up their consequences. Having constructed the noble architecture of love with his precious vows, he now received his own message back from his mistress: 'If words are what matter, trust them and not what you see.'

If lying is what indicates that one is within the dimension of language, what about those creatures that seem to deceive yet don't speak? If wolves can lie, wouldn't this in fact demonstrate that language and lying are not as bound up as we think? But this is not quite the case. If a certain female firefly can mimic the precopulatory flash pattern of a female of another species to attract and then devour the male of that same species or if a creature can assume the colourings of its habitat or cover its tracks, does this really count as lying? They are certainly examples of deceit, but deceit and the lie become different the moment that one is in a world of real language. As Lacan argued, the difference resides in what separates a bluff from a double bluff. When the 101 Dalmations are trying to escape from their captors, they cover up their tracks in the snow, but a hunted man may leave his tracks just as they are, to lead his pursuers into error: seeing the tracks, they may assume that the tracks are false and that they are being bluffed. What characterises the double bluff is that the subjectivity of the pursuer is taken into account in the orchestration of deceit: or, more precisely, the fact that the pursuer is someone who speaks, who inhabits a world of signs. He is assumed to be someone who expects to be deceived, which is different from someone who simply is deceived, someone who is aware that a sign can always mean more than one thing. The psychoanalyst Ernest Jones once wrote a paper called

'Persons in Dreams Disguised as Themselves', but when one is dealing with animals, such a multiplication of layers would hardly be possible. The sensitivity to this difference can become a matter not simply of intellectual curiosity but of national interest. When a German aircraft crash-landed in Belgium in January 1940, the officer on board appeared to be in possession of a complete set of plans for Germany's offensive against the Allies. He tried desperately to set fire to the documents, but was captured before he was able to do so. And yet the success of this interception was only dampened by the theory of signs: assuming that a map could mean both itself and its opposite, the Allied intelligence staff decided that it was a deliberate deception, and thus they chose not to adjust their own strategies in any significant way. Although it would have been bizarre to deceive the Allies into expecting an attack through Belgium as detailed in the plans, the assumption that a bluff was in operation won over their military knowledge. Formulated in the terms of the well-known joke, their attitude would have been improved if they had elevated bluff into double bluff: 'Why are you telling me you are going to Belgium, making me believe that you are in fact going somewhere else, when I know that you are indeed going to Belgium?'

If the lie has its place in the forging of subjectivity, it is equally present in the relation to others, and Lacan went as far as to call it 'the characteristic feature of intersubjectivity'. This seems strange, given that intersubjectivity implies a link to other people whereas lying would involve keeping to oneself, guarding some knowledge which is not circulated. But the remark shows, in fact, what intersubjectivity is really about: if you assume the one you address can deceive you, that means you are not simply talking to yourself. It shows that you are speaking to someone you really don't know, which is what separates the intrasubjective dialogue with oneself from the intersubjective link to the other. When it happens that a man spends a whole evening telling a woman about his car, that would be an example of a relation which is not intersubjective: he might as well be talking to himself, even if the woman doesn't complain since she might be attracted to the rare spectacle of a man talking with passion about something. This is also the way in which Lacan separates intersubjectivity from the field of science. The key factor to physical science, he said at one point, is that we don't assume that behind the phenomena we study, there is someone using them. They may be created by a god, but they do not deceive us with purpose: atoms don't get together before a big experiment to decide on how they will behave to produce the required illusion. Or rather, they may for all we know be doing that, but to do science we have to exclude this possibility. There is a basic act of faith here, regardless of how much we may believe that performing an experiment generates its 'own' data or creates its 'own' reality. However dependent such results may be on the many layers of the scientific programme in question, we do not attribute subjectivity to the objects in question, we do not assume a will to deceive.

There is a fine line here, discussed by Lacan, between science and paranoia. Elaborating a scientific programme means supposing that there is some knowledge out there which hasn't been accessed, a law of nature that would make sense of anomalous phenomena. If atoms, for example, behave in a particular way, it might be possible to formulate a law governing their behaviour, thereby producing a knowledge but not, evidently, a knowing subject. Paranoia also supposes this kind of knowledge in the outside world, but adds to it the figure of the knower. The clouds may be moving in particular patterns and the traffic in particular configurations, and paranoia involves the passage from this initial observation of an order to the positing that this order is the result of some subjective agency behind it: they move in this or that way because an evil genius has willed it. It is this positing of a subject which separates early Christianity from Gnosticism: while both recognise the existence of evil in the world, the next step of assuming a subject to it is shirked by Christianity. Whereas Gnostic thought deduces from the presence of good and evil in the world the presence of two deities, one good and one evil, Christianity's commitment to monotheism could not allow this. Instead, we have the one God and, to explain the evil, the story of the Fall.

If it is language that introduces the distinction between the true and the false, these two qualities are complicated the moment that people start speaking. A lie can become the same thing as the truth, just as ignorance can be the same thing as knowledge. When Joseph Surface is visited by his guardian Sir Peter Teazle in *The School for Scandal*, he quickly takes advantage of a screen to hide Sir Peter's wife whom he is in the process of seducing. As Sir Peter voices his suspicions of Lady Teazle, the comedy of the scene is generated by the shifting reference of the words he employs: as he speaks of 'the person' who has designs on his wife, the audience know that this refers to Mr Surface, while Sir Peter thinks it refers to Joseph's brother Charles. What may be false regarding Charles may be true for Joseph, and if Sir Peter's words about 'the person' are taken seriously, they are thus true at one level and false at another. Literally, he is speaking the truth, but he just doesn't know what he is saying.

If such situations are frequent in comedy, they are no less so off the stage, and especially so not only when someone is misinformed but when a deliberate falsehood is being spun. If you invent a story to deceive, it is certain that this story will itself embody an unconscious truth. Questioned as to his whereabouts the previous night, a teenager admits to his parents that he had been in the company of woman. Wishing consciously to withhold the lady's name, he responds to their request for further details with an invented name, a baptism which becomes troubling when he suddenly realises that he has chosen the middle name of his mother. The unconscious desire thus finds its niche in the space opened up by invention.

The Hungarian analyst Michael Balint received a patient who proceeded to tell him a long and complicated story about his life. By the end of the first consultation, Balint admits that he needs more time to get a picture of the case, and so another session is arranged. As he continues his story at their next meeting, Balint interrupts him with the confession that he is still clueless. The patient takes a deep breath, Balint tells us, and says, 'At last – a sincere man.' His entire story, from his name to the list of his nervous symptoms, had been invented, as a test, he says, to find a truthful man to whom he could disclose his secrets. The other specialists he had seen had all been too quick to understand and offer advice and prescriptions. Balint points out to him that his method of testing is rather expensive and no doubt tiresome. But in fact, what psychoanalysis shows is that this invented story probably contained some crucial unconscious truth. The distance which this patient put between himself and the story is perhaps an alibi, even if the sequence introduces the further problem of the relation of that speaker to his speech. A deliberate lie may be identical with truth. In Sophocles' *Trachiniae*, the wife of Heracles sends her unfaithful husband a robe dipped in what she believes to be a love potion. She conceals this effort to regain his affections with a lie, telling him that she made the robe so that if he returned home safely he could present himself to the gods freshly clad for a sacrifice. She is unaware, however, that the love potion is in fact a poison, and thus when Heracles dons the robe he will be presenting himself to the gods in a way very different from what her lie had implied: the sacrifice will be himself. Her lie thus tells the truth: it is formally identical with a truth, perhaps one which shortcircuited her conscious understanding. Confronted with the infidelity of her husband, when she receives the robe from someone who is obviously hostile to Heracles, she chooses to maintain a belief in its reparative virtues: when perhaps she knows only too well, at another level, that this love potion is a poison and that each of her kisses is a death wish. Her words are telling the truth in more ways than she thinks.

A clinical sequence can make this relation of the speaker to his speech more precise. A man recounts two dreams from the same night. In the first, he is in a supermarket and slips a little piece of cake into his mouth before attempting to leave casually. The manager stops him in the street and now both of them set out in search of a stolen car, even though the subject knows perfectly well where this car is parked. As the feigned search continues, his anxiety becomes intolerable and he tries to flee but cannot run fast enough. The second dream takes the form of the single and peculiar sentence, 'I am a thief of wood.' This isolated phrase produces an immediate association, forming part of the dream material, to the anecdote of a man suspected by his employer of stealing something. As he leaves the factory where he works every evening, his wheelbarrow is searched systematically: nothing is found, until at last it is understood that he is stealing wheelbarrows. As he describes the two dreams, he uses the same word to describe the manager of the supermarket in the first dream and the employer at the factory in the anecdote. Now, without going into the details of all the associations offered, what interests us is the presence in these dreams of two kinds of theft. Firstly, there is the search for a stolen object, the car in the first dream, the objects contained in the wheelbarrow in the second, and then there is the real theft, incarnated in the first dream by the man himself, with cake in his mouth, and in the second dream by the wheelbarrow. The crucial moment in the anecdote is when the wheelbarrow emerges not as the name of a set of objects – those supposedly hidden inside it – but as a set itself. If we call the fictitious set of objects W, we can call the latter the set of the set of W. And it is exactly at this moment of revelation that the wheelbarrow was always empty that it becomes the set of the empty set. An object that isn't being counted – the wheelbarrow – suddenly starts to count as an object itself. The subject does his best to get the other to look inside the wheelbarrow instead of looking at the wheelbarrow itself, just as, in the first dream, he tries to persuade the manager to search for the stolen car rather than the stolen object which is even closer to home – the cake. This may appear to be an abstract analysis, void of clinical import, yet what it shows is something at the heart of the experience of analysis, the role of speaking.

The patient was someone who talked a great deal, offering psychological explanations of his associations and the episodes in his life with little reserve. Despite the many problems and insecurities he complained of, the one thing he felt sure of was his speech. This was the one constant he felt he could rely on, and in his memories of childhood it formed a particularly important link with the mother. It was what allowed him, he said time and time again, 'to have his cake and eat it'. And this cake, as the first dream shows, is not just in his mouth, it is stolen. Distinguishing the two different logical levels in the dream sequence shows the topography of this relation to speech: this man would speak about the most unpleasant things to do his good work as a patient, yet the one thing which he had to keep out of the analytic dynamic was putting into question not what he said but the form of his speech itself. Speaking could produce many meanings, but what really mattered was the meaning of speaking, just as in the second dream it is the wheelbarrow and not the search for what is inside it that counts. The sentence 'I am a thief of wood' thus demands to be reformulated 'I am a thief of speech', a speech the subject wanted to take from his father but without paying the price. The wheelbarrows, in his description, were made of wood, and his father's manner of expressing himself was, in his words, 'wooden'. Shortly after recounting the dreams, he arrived for his appointment with the peculiar idea that his presence then and there would stop me from noticing that he had not come to his session on the previous day: his presence at this session would be his alibi. His speaking with such honesty now would cover his guilty tracks regarding the previous day, exactly as in the dreams we have discussed. His speech and the wheelbarrow shared the same logical structure: to look for what's inside, while ignoring the form itself. This structure was linked with the decision to enter analysis in the first place. Analysis consisted, as this patient knew well, of speaking, yet it was the relation to speaking which emerged as a key problem. If he had always assumed he could count on his speech, he now inferred, in analysis, that he could count on it even more, since that was what analysis was all about. It was, after all, a talking cure. The tension was between the demand to be relieved of suffering and the fact that the method he had chosen to do this would leave the dynamic that generated the suffering untouched. And, as it turned out, the most important moments in the treatment were exactly those when the power of speech collapsed, the moments when his skills at persuasion failed him and he was not met with any acknowledgement. The greatest threat was the threat of doing away with the validity of the word. At these moments, the relation to speech became clear: if what the patient was saying lost its grounding, if it became worthless, he was left with the form of speaking itself, and the emptiness of this form would evoke the powerlessness that lay behind it. The meaning of his speech thus lost its priority to the problem of the use of his speech, which had taken on its value in childhood as the privileged way of responding to an unbearable anxiety. It had taken on the value of what the patient had, and questioning it would thus introduce all the problems of loss and frustration that made up the foundations of his life.

This clinical vignette invites comparison with one of Lacan's most celebrated clinical commentaries, the case of the Fresh Brains Man. This patient had been in analysis with Melanie Klein's daughter, Melitta Schmideberg, in the early 1930s, and then with Ernst Kris, who presented a short account of the case in 1948. Lacan commented on the material at several moments of his seminar, focusing always on a particularly fascinating sequence. The patient is a young scientist who has a respectable academic post yet is unable to advance due to a difficulty in publishing any of his research. He is tormented by the idea that he is a plagiarist and is systematically hampered in his career by this worry. The ideas he feels under pressure to use are frequently those of a close friend of his, a scholar whose office is adjacent to his own and with whom he has long daily conversations. One day he shows up in Kris' office and, with visible elation, tells his analyst that he has just discovered an old volume in the library which contains the germ of the thesis he is just now preparing to publish. Kris questions him carefully, and then assures him that he is not a plagiarist: his own thesis is properly his own given the conventions of academic research. It was the scholar friend, in fact, who was the real plagiarist as it was he who borrowed the patient's ideas and repeated them without due acknowledgement. Kris goes on to tell the patient about his wishes to take and to steal, which have become connected to the world of ideas. Only the ideas of others were truly interesting, ideas that could be taken: hence the taking, Kris tells him, had to be engineered. After this long interpretation, the patient is silent for a moment and then tells Kris that every day, after his session, he walks down a narrow street near the analyst's office, searching the menus for his favourite dish: fresh brains.

How can this information be understood? Like every surprising disclosure in an analysis, the question of its meaning cannot be separated from that of its timing. Why was it at that moment that he chose to tell Kris? As Lacan argued, it is a particular type of response to the analyst's interpretation, but what message is it carrying? When the same patient had been in analysis with Melitta Schmideberg, he had spoken of his theft of sweets and books during puberty, and she had explained his concern with plagiarism as a way of escaping the drive to steal via inhibition. If what he really wants is to steal things for himself, by blocking his own progress with the thought that he's plagiarising, he defends against the dangerous impulse. Stealing derives, she thinks, from the oral impulse to incorporate, to swallow things up. Whereas Schmideberg evokes practically no clinical material, Kris adds a number of details. The grandfather was a man esteemed for his intellectual powers, while the father seemed to abdicate from the field of ideas. The patient remembers fishing trips with his father, centring on the image of the contest as to who could catch the biggest fish, and the memory of exchanging and comparing fishes is recalled with many details. Commenting on the case, the psychoanalyst Bernard Burgoyne has pointed out that Lacan links the adjective used to describe the quality of the fish, 'big' (*gross*) with the prefix of the title of the 'grandfather' (*Grossvater*). Hence it might appear obvious to interpret the intellectual inhibition in terms of an identification with the father, a man who retires from the arena of competition with the grandfather and an abdication from the world of ideas. But this is not the only interpretation.

What interests Lacan in the case is first of all the question of desire. Kris is telling the patient, 'Look, you're not a plagiarist,' to which he responds with the story of the fresh brains. The information thus seems to be a corrective to the analyst, indicating to him that 'being a plagiarist' has nothing to do with reality. Kris' interpretation relied on supposedly factual information about academic procedure and the real content of the two works in question, but the patient's message is that it is not at the level of any 'shared reality' that the problem is to be situated: it is at the level of discourse, of language, that one is or isn't a plagiarist. And, as the material makes quite clear, the fear of plagiarism that the patient complains of conceals nothing less than the desire to be a plagiarist. It may be noted here that nearly all of the many commentators on this case repeat a gesture which is linked with the material they are studying: although Kris' intervention indeed appeals to 'reality', he never says that he went and read through the book that was supposedly plagiarised from. All he says is that prior to interpreting, he engaged in 'a process of extended scrutiny', which might have taken the form of a detailed series of questions. The almost universal assumption that he went and read the book himself is curious: apart from being false, it suggests, in its distortion, that Kris is really quite close to the list of characters involved in the battle of books which the case is about. In a footnote, he says that 'without being consciously aware of it' he was following the example of Helene Deutsch in the way he examined the patient, thereby adding one more name to the list of borrowers. If he had followed instead the example of Pope Gregory VII, not only would he not have read the book, he would have taken the care to destroy it properly. The Vatican library became sadly depleted of so many classical manuscripts when Gregory became aware of the free use his favourite author Augustine had made of the work of Varro: he chose to destroy the texts of this Roman writer rather than see his beloved church father convicted of plagiarism. If Kris had been so inclined, he could have purloined the book in question, but the man so eager to be a plagiarist would no doubt have found others, and his analyst would have been obliged to lay waste to the world's libraries. Kris, being a civilised man, would never have done such a thing, and even if he had entertained the thought, he would have been well aware of the lesson learnt by those who have tried: that it is in fact much easier to burn authors than to burn books.

When Lacan returns to a discussion of the case a year or so later, it is from a slightly different angle. The fresh brains are now described as a 'renewal of the symptom', in the sense that where the plagiarism was concerned with the devouring of ideas, it is now a question of the devouring of brains. The brains are substituted for the ideas, to keep the basic structure of the symptom intact. But, as Lacan adds, the key to the sequence is to understand that symbols and ideas don't ever belong to anybody: in the world of language, there's no symbolic property, an insight that illuminates the clinical material in a new way. What matters now is the distinction between the content of the ideas which are supposedly stolen and the field of ideas itself. Whereas Kris had focused on the first of these, assessing whether plagiarism there had been in terms of the actual real-life content of the patient's thesis, what he misses, we could say, is the wheelbarrow itself, the form of speech as it exists for this patient. Hence Lacan can offer a diagnosis, in his next discussion of the material: it's not that the patient isn't stealing anything, as Kris held, but rather that what he is stealing is nothing. The diagnosis is thus, Lacan argues, mental anorexia, a refusal not of food but of ideas, or, more precisely, of the desire which is inhabited by ideas. Whereas Kris searches for the stolen object in the meaning of the texts written by others, he fails to see that the real plagiarism is in the form of the object itself, the fact that for this man something can only have a value if it belongs to someone else.

It is this which puts the subject in a position of what he feels, consciously, as inauthenticity. And if the idea always belongs to someone else, how can one take up a place within it except by refusing, as Kris' patient does, or, perhaps, by deliberate deception. The diagnosis of anorexia, strange as it may seem, is thus perfectly logical, if it is understood in the sense of a symbolic refusal. When a child refuses to eat, it is often clear that the refusal has nothing to do with the quality or the content of the food itself: it is a symbolic action, which takes on a meaning in the context of the response of the parent who is trying to do the feeding. Just as it is often said that a child needs someone to eat *for*, we can add that it also needs someone *not* to eat for. When that person is the mother, the effect is guaranteed, as there are few things more difficult for a mother to witness than the failure to eat of her child. The lack that the child incarnates will resonate in her at the deepest levels and confront her with her failure to satisfy her child. But what Kris' material shows is something more precise, how giving a value to whatever belongs to someone else does not make one's own position any easier: what the man cannot do, in this case, is to have something. And, as the material shows, this is where he has lodged his unconscious enjoyment: he is desperate not to have something that belongs to himself. The problem, of course, is that maintaining this position indeed gives him the idea that he *does*: the satisfaction is in the subjectivity, which is embodied in the refusal. Instead of aiming to *have* ideas, he enjoys by *being* someone without them. When Lacan suggests that Kris tell the patient that he is stealing nothing, this aims to upset the way in which he is clinging to his 'not having'. It is therefore more than a mere irony that Nelson, the man who had the greatest interest in what belonged to another man (Lady Hamilton) should steal something from his headmaster's orchard as a child (some pears) and yet refuse to eat the stolen fruit himself, distributing it instead amongst the other boys. It shows that what he had, he stole, and yet it never quite belonged to him. That's why in his love life there are always more than two players present: Emma Hamilton came with her husband Sir William, and even in the privacy of their correspondence he is obliged to invent fictional third parties to multiply the characters once more. The less a man can have, the more people there will be around, either as the ones to have in his place or as those who must be shown to have nothing.

The intention to deceive has often perplexed scholars trying to account for the strange behaviour of literary history's greatest fibber, Odysseus. Throughout his adventures, he concocts stories to deceive, usually with the aim of either gaining information or saving himself from some turbulence. But sometimes his lying is more bizarre. He may have disguised his identity on returning to Ithaca to test the fidelity of his wife Penelope, but why then does he choose to mask himself from his aged father Laertes? This behaviour appeared so strange that several ancients wanted to end the *Odyssey* at Book 23, before the deceit in question. The Greek hero's untruths may even be at the source of the famous paradox of the lying Cretan. If a Cretan tells you 'All Cretans are liars', does that statement count as a lie itself? The complications of this conceit are obvious, and have been much discussed by the philosophers, yet its origins remain opaque. It is Odysseus, however, who, in one of the many big lies of the *Odyssey*, claims to Eumaeus that he has come from Crete. Although this may enlighten us as to a possible source of the connection between liars and Cretans, it does make things more difficult: if the problem seemed to turn around Cretans who were liars, there is now the new dimension of liars who claim to be Cretans. To be Cretan doesn't make you a liar, but to say that you're Cretan does. Thus anyone who says that 'All Cretans are liars', in asserting their own Cretan origins, puts lie upon lie. Until the Cretan gene is identified, which would dispense with the necessity of the claim to be Cretan, perhaps philosophers may examine this puzzle, and even add to it the study of what it might mean to promise to be Cretan.

Now, rather than seeing the lie to Laertes as yet one more example of the cunning tendencies of the hero, perhaps its position at the end of the series of lies is important in itself. Odysseus fibs to all and sundry, to Athene, to Eumaeus, to Antinous and to Penelope, but the last lie is to his father. As his story is the story of a journey home, a departure and then a return, doesn't this suggest that the last lie is in fact the same as the first? The problem with Odysseus is that, in his relation with the parental lineage, there is a basic untruth. When his nurse places him on the knees of his grandfather Autolycus and suggests a name meaning 'Child of Prayer', he chooses 'Man of Odium' instead. Autolycus was notorious for lying and deceit, and his choice of name translates this malignity, condemning the boy to a life *in between two names*. This passion for being someone else is echoed in the famous scene in which, to deceive the one-eyed ogre Polyphemus, he names himself 'Nobody'. When the wounded giant cries out for help and is asked who is responsible for his complaint, the 'Nobody' of his reply persuades the other ogres that not much is afoot, and Odysseus and his band can exit. But rather than seeing this 'Nobody' as the artfully constructed response of the hero, introduced to further a plan of escape, why not understand it instead as more in the nature of a slip of the tongue, the emergence of an element in speech which reveals a truth? The ogre may have only one eye, but the hero has always got more than one name. And having more than one name is no different from having no name at all.

This question of identity provided Lacan with a surprising definition of the neurotic: someone with no name. Contrary to the popular view of the neurotic as someone infatuated with their own qualities, believing, as it were, only in their own name, Lacan claimed that the only person to really have a name is the mad person. Napoleon was not mad for the simple reason that he was never quite sure of being Napoleon, always worrying about whether or not he could live up to his name, anxious to hear reports about the man he was supposed to be, and comparing his own line of descent with that of his councillors. Without this uncertainty, Talleyrand would never have taken the risk, at a party in Warsaw, of putting a napkin over his arm when his general asked him for a glass of lemonade. The secretary of state's more aristocratic descent was temporarily abandoned as he took on the appearance of a waiter, playing nicely on Napoleon's insecurities. In contrast, the certainty of madness opposes itself to the 'never being quite sure' of the neurotic, and the mad person who tells the world he is Christ will experience no doubt: hence the futility of attempts to persuade him that he is in fact someone else.

But why should the neurotic be thus nameless? Lacan says that he is nameless due to what he calls his 'strong ego', an ironic expression aimed as a barb to the many practitioners who think that the goal, rather than the initial problem, of neurosis is to produce a strong ego. One might then assume that having a strong ego means having a strong identity, being really convinced about who one is. But once again, the phrase is deceptive. The ego is not a pole of fixed identity as such, but refers always to someone else, the borrowed image of another person or, in this case, a kind of annex to the desire of the mother, in the way that a child will assume an image that it believes the mother is interested in. Having a strong ego thus means being suspended in a strong way on the desire of someone else. And being suspended on the desire of someone else means lacking an independent identity, what an Anglo-Saxon writer might call a 'failure of separation'. Which, as everyone agrees, is the cause of much suffering. When Peter Sellers went on the Parkinson show, he could only make his initial appearance dressed up as a German soldier. Called upon to appear as 'himself', he had no choice but to appear as 'another'. Rather than seeing this as just a device to delight the studio audience, the passion for disguise invites another interpretation, one which is linked to the detail of his history. As a child, he would watch his mother have slides projected on to her, dressing her in one identity after another, from Florence Nightingale and Queen Victoria to the Statue of

Liberty. Her son, the specialist of multiple roles, was often unrecognisable even to those who were closest to him, so great was the elasticity and brilliance of his identifications. This talent for having identities was, as he knew, the same thing as not having one. Like Quilty in *Lolita*, he is everyone and no one at the same time, the master of disguise who, when undisguised, can only slide towards another mask. There is thus no contradiction between the specialist of multiple roles and the solitary gardener of *Being There*: being there, in the place of what is lacking to the mother, is the same as being everywhere.

We find a contrasting example of someone not being there, this time with the idea of registering limits, in Edmund Gosse's Victorian memoir *Father and Son*. He describes a dream in which he is galloping through a kind of infinite space, bound hand and foot to a horse like Mazeppa. It seemed to him as if a terrible force was driving him on, but he knew he would never reach the goal in the distance. This goal was a strange one: it consisted of the ruby-coloured letters of the word 'carmine'. Gosse explains that his father was fond of watercolour painting, and that the most precious of his paints was an intense crimson, the carmine that only the father was permitted to use. We can recall that Mazeppa was a famous cossack, punished for his affair with a married woman by being bound to a wild horse by her husband and driven into a lonely steppe where he was expected to perish. This detail confirms the oedipal signification of the dream, involving as it does a married woman, a husband and a contender for the woman. The interest of this dream is in the clarity of its symbolic accent: the carmine functions as the signifier of what is desired the most, the limit point which he cannot reach and the marker of a prohibition. It demonstrates the fixing of the oedipal barrier at a symbolic level: the sacrifice of an enjoyment linked to the mother, incarnated in a pure linguistic form, the ruby letters which index his exclusion.

❦

Many initiation ceremonies conclude in giving a new name to the initiate, often after some kind of ritual beating: an adolescent, for example, has to run the course of a line of men who club him as he passes. After that he can take on a name. The neurotic, in contrast, is someone who, in his namelessness, might spend his whole life being clubbed, never getting to the end of the line when the symbolic act of naming takes place. What he loves is his namelessness, and no amount of suffering can tear him away from it. Kris' patient, the Fresh Brains Man, put the name of others before his own in his passion for the idea of plagiarism: there was always another name there first. As he tried to show Kris, it was this idea he was attached to: whatever his analyst tried to tell him, he didn't want to sacrifice the idea of being a plagiarist, in other words, of his namelessness. It was this 'failure' that was so close to him. The interpretation that Lacan suggested – 'You're stealing nothing' – would have aimed at putting this commitment in question: on one level, it implies that there is no value in his supposed plagiarism, and at another, it evokes the nothing, the absence beyond the series of imaginary objects, the big fishes, he wants to take. Where the patient basked in his namelessness and evidently enjoyed his position of not having something, the interpretation would have aimed at the point where there really is no name, where there really is nothing to steal, the phallus not as an imaginary object (a big fish) but as a symbolic one (a big lack).

This difference between what one wants to get and what one cannot have can give us some clues about the links between promising, deception and the question of identity.

Where Edmund Gosse was confronted with a symbolic limit, indicating what he could never have, the Fresh Brains Man was more interested in getting things. Since he couldn't succeed in really having something, he did the next best thing and shifted his enjoyment to the idea of not having something. The problem is that these operations involve different registers: you can try to obtain as many objects as you like, but the real cause of your search is an object which can't be 'had' in the same way. That's why shopping is only a transitory solution to anxiety. An object might provide you with the illusion that a lack has been filled, but this is hardly the same thing as having taken on board the symbolic limit that we find illustrated so finely in Gosse's dream. In the same way, a child might try to give a lot to its mother, and then realise that it can never give everything. If the mother seems interested in something which is not just her child, manifested for example in her absences, the son or daughter can try to capture her with a series of games and images, tricks and deceptions designed to deceive her. He can disappear and then reveal himself, make her worry about his whereabouts or his safety, utter the sweetest sentences or refuse to give her a moment's peace. With the realisation, as Lacan puts it, that he does not have the absolute weapon, a whole range of images and illusions are brought into play, games of seduction which aim at giving the child a special value for her. But these are based on the fundamental failure of being the only object of her pleasure. Which is why, later in life, when a man is seducing a woman, he may have the feeling that he is not being himself, that he is living a lie, even when he is doing nothing but telling the truth. As Helene Deutsch pointed out, many people feel like impostors or fakes even when what they are up to is perfectly legitimate. And it is well known that many men have more interest in the process of seduction than in its consequences. When a woman, in being 'forward', deprives the man of the actual process of seduction, he may become deeply hostile to her. The adventure leading up to the 'conquest' will matter more than the conquest of the night itself, showing that what the man has to demonstrate is his ability to carry out the great deception of his first failed romance with the mother. He'd only tried to captivate her, after all, because he realised that she was captivated by something that wasn't identical with himself. That's why it is often said that men are less interested in hearing a woman say to them 'I love you' than 'I'm proud of you', as it registers what he has managed to achieve.

Indeed, many men find the real attraction of a sexual encounter in being able to produce some reaction in their partner: what matters for them is to succeed in being the cause of a woman's enjoyment, in other words, to become what is necessary for her, what completes her. A man may have no conscious interest whatsoever in a woman's breasts, only in being able to make her nipples erect. Without touching her in some particular place, she wouldn't react in the way that she does. Thus the sexual act becomes for the man the field of a demonstration, a proof, which is why sex is sometimes described as a virility test. The key here is to understand that this proof is based on a failure, and the seduction which might precede the act of love is formally identical to a deception, since the initial incentive to seduce is always one that misfired, a sense that one is lacking, that one does not have what it takes. That's why many men carry on seducing when they know perfectly well that it is not good for them: promiscuity becomes a symptom. It is the first disappointment that makes each truth uttered in the seduction a lie, since one is offering something based on the unsuitability, at the start, of oneself.

At the root of romance is always a romance that failed, that didn't work, as the child 'didn't have what it takes'. There is a failure to be something or to have something. And this is perhaps the reason why men sometimes behave in such crazy ways. As a rule, when a man witnesses what he assumes to be the deception of a woman, a woman's being taken in, the result is a fury which surpasses the concerns of a companion. And all the more so if the man is himself deceiving the woman in question in the first place. When the situation involves a rival competing for the woman's affections, the real panic for the man is often less a sense of the rival's superiority than, as Reik pointed out, the idea that the loved one *sees* superiority in him. In other words, she might be taken in by the rival, which strikes a chord very close to home: if she is taken in by the rival, that means that she was taken in by him in the first place. The jealous motif here thus concerns the man's own value, the fact that his accomplishments are based, literally, on nothing. He can continue deceiving the woman, but the moment another party comes along who introduces the same situation, he loses all faith. The hostility to the woman, in such cases, is thus linked to the fragility of his own position, but only when it is reflected in her relation to another man. Otherwise, how could one explain the fact that so many men search for one single sign from a woman: her slightly ironic smile, indicating that, despite his parade, she has seen through all his pretences.

Is this an answer to the question of why love doesn't last? If the relation to a woman is based on an original failure, will a man then abandon his partner with the realisation that he has failed to complete her too? This might suggest that he will then try to find another partner with whom to act out the same scenario all over again. Neurotics, as the psychoanalyst Edmund Bergler once said, are like people who take the same gramophone record with them to every party: what interests them is less an encounter with the new than the perpetuation of the same basic situation. But there must be a difference between those people who are determined to experience one failed romance after another and those who are content with just one. What they demand from a relationship might be a bit different, and hence one could hope that when such people meet each other, they are not reading the same self-help book. We could contrast here the deceit which a man might employ in his attempts to live up to some image with a woman and the sort of almost obsessive honesty which seems to characterise many seductions. But honesty is in fact a big problem, especially for those who seem to have no choice but to tell the truth. If erudites have used up so much ink trying to elucidate the lies of Odysseus, we have to tackle the more difficult question of why it is that some people tell the truth, not just now and then, but with a compulsion. Heine was always suspicious of Rousseau's so-called confessions, and in his *Memoirs* he expresses his scepticism as to Jean Jacques' theft of a ribbon, which supposedly caused the unjust dismissal of a chambermaid. Beyond this appeal to truth, the poet saw another crime which was not mentioned. Likewise, the heartless banishment of the children of Thérèse Levasseur to a foundling hospital does not count, for Heine, as the confession of a cruel father, but rather conceals the more probable crime of not having been their father at all. What the confession reveals is that a further detail is not being confessed, and this structure is familiar in psychoanalytic practice. A patient will reveal something about himself which is embarrassing and unpleasant, yet which is only confessed in order to throw the analysis off the track of some other element. That's why there is no real confession in analysis: each admission only evokes the point where something else is not being said. When George Washington told his dad that he had cut down the fruit tree, he made his confession no doubt because there was something else of which he was far guiltier. Maybe he could have then continued masturbating in peace. If he had included himself in his confession about the fruit tree, there was something else, an unknown act or desire, from which he had, in Samuel Goldwyn's happy expression, included himself out.

If deceit includes one out, honesty, it would seem, includes one in. To make a confession implies that we take responsibility for what we say, that we include ourselves in our words, the opposite of what happens in lying. When someone tells a lie, they are separate from what they say: they are not included. But this, as we have seen, is not as simple as it seems. A deliberate lie may tell an unconscious truth. If inclusion is not an adequate criterion to test the true and the false, it may well be the measure of something else. In an old intelligence test, the child who says 'I've got three brothers, Paul, Ernest and myself' loses a few points. By including himself in the concept 'brother', he has shown his backwardness. But, as Lacan pointed out in his discussion of this example, what it shows is less backwardness than the process of being included in language itself. To operate in a linguistic world, one has to be counted there at the level of concepts: the problems would emerge when one failed to be included. Many of the games that children play revolve around this idea of being counted: skipping, for example, is about counting oneself, and its gymnastics are orchestrated around rhymes and words. Skippers have to skip in time, or they become caught out, separated from the rhyme. Similarly, there are the games which involve a formula being recited, where each word will designate one of the children until one is left out. 'Raggle taggle dish cloth torn in two out goes you,' for example, in which a sequence of words both includes some of the players and then designates one as 'it'. One could also evoke the many games in which uttering a particular word makes the players stop in their tracks. These games demonstrate the operations of language as they have taken hold of its speakers, showing how the relation to speech means that one is both 'in' and 'out'.

Language gives us a place and at the same time excludes us. At the end of the film *Dumb and Dumber*, two cretins find themselves in the middle of the American countryside, having lost their woman, their wealth and their employment. Solitary and alone, they have nothing in the way of positive attributes. Suddenly a tour coach pulls up beside them filled with ravishingly beautiful women. The doors open and their representative emerges, informing them that the group of beauties need 'a couple of guys' to help grease down their bodies before each competition on their National Bikini Tour. And she then enquires in a suggestive tone whether they might just happen to know the men for the job. One of the cretins, whether he is the dumb or the dumber one is unclear, ponders for a moment and then, pointing, says, Yes, they're sure to find two guys if they follow the road to the next town. As the coach disappears and the puzzled beauties desert them, he realises his enormous mistake: he has pointed them in the wrong direction since the town is to the left and not to the right. What this example shows is that dumbness, if such a thing exists, is less the result of inclusion in a concept than of the failure to include oneself in a concept: as the beauty queen had referred to 'a couple of guys', they had failed to include themselves in this concept. For them, it always referred to someone else. Which brings us back to the theme of promises, since a promise is the one part of speech where we refer explicitly to the fact that we are including ourselves in what we say.

❦

Philosophers who have turned their attention to promises have described them as speech acts or, in the terms of John Austin, performatives. A performative is a part of language that does something, like a vow, an oath or a pledge. It is the act of speech itself which performs an action: in the latter examples, that of committing the speaker to something. As performatives were studied, it became apparent that they could not really be separated from the rest of speech, since all speech is actually doing something. Whatever you say, some action is taking place. The interest of the more explicit performatives is less as an isolated part of language then as an instance where a special focus is moved to the act of speaking, an emphasis on the way a speaker is included in his or her words. The vows of marriage would constitute a privileged example of this, where one is committed and betrothed as one speaks, rather than seeing the words as simply a description of something. It is not normally possible to go through a marriage ceremony and then claim that, as one didn't mean what one said, one is freed from the commitments involved. Uttering the words has a binding effect, and in uttering them one is included, whether one likes it or not. A reality is created, once again, just from words.

Some people don't like the idea of going through with these vows. They may decide never to get married, even though they live with their loved one, or, on making the decision to take the vows, they may fail to appear on their wedding day. In *Four Weddings and a Funeral*, Charles (Hugh Grant) decides, at least formally, to get married, and then commits the inexcusable act of interrupting the marriage vows on the very day of the wedding. It seems that he prefers an American lady, Carrie, played by Andie MacDowell, and it is she who apparently saves him from the kind of marriage people make when it gets late. Now, if this film had simply kept to the standard narrative of the man who avoids getting married until he finds true love, it would no doubt have been much less successful, despite the charms of its stars. To explain its amazing success, its two singularities have to be noted: the presence of a funeral and the character of Hugh Grant's brother, who is unable to speak. On an immediate level, this last feature of the film is the easiest to account for. When Charles pursues Carrie and confronts her on the Embankment, he tells her that, 'in the words of David Cassidy', he loves her and then asks her to . . . without being able to finish his sentence. When it comes to saying these things of the heart, he can only use the words of someone else, just as in the film's narrative he is forever at the weddings of other people, rather than his own. This inability to speak is reflected in the dumbness of the brother, and it is thus necessary for the brother to intervene, on Charles' wedding day, in order to allow him to speak out. Yet, as the ending makes clear, his problems are not over yet: when he is reconciled with Carrie in the final scene, he says to her, 'Will you agree not to marry me?', to which she replies 'I do.' Even now, after the realisation that he will be faithful to his true love, he cannot say the words, and uses instead the Freudian mechanism of denegation, articulating a positive as a negative, inserting the 'not', perhaps, as a sign that his doubts are not over.

Charles' sentence belongs to the same series as the 'I will never not be indebted to you' of Bette Davis' hateful daughter. This energetic woman would write *My Mother's Keeper*, one of the most scalding books ever published by a child about its parent, and even when she received a substantial cash transfer from her mother, her letter of thanks could only articulate itself in double negative. The more negatives there are, as Freud showed, the more the unconscious dynamics are at work, so that a 'not' can become identical with an affirmation. As a recent book of interviews with prominent scientists makes clear: when questioned gently by the interviewer, they all speak of the paternal influence on their careers, and their respect and admiration for the father. Except for one, the only exception, who chooses to begin the interview by stating that he wishes it to be known that his father has had no influence on him whatsoever, absolutely none at all, zero, never learnt anything from him etc. In other words, out of all of those interviewed in the book, it is only here that we can be sure of a very passionate link to the father. The multiplication of denials evokes exactly their contrary.

Now, if the brother in *Four Weddings* points to the motif of not being able to speak, his relation with Charles invites the viewer to ask the further question, Speak about what? Charles is an odd sort, at home with his gang of friends but unable to sustain a relation with a woman. When he helps Carrie choose a wedding dress, the expedition replaces a rendezvous with his brother. And later, at the church, it is the brother who interrupts the proceedings when the vicar asks if there is any impediment to going ahead with the marriage: in sign language he says that he suspects the groom loves someone else. If we take this last proposition seriously, Charles indeed loves someone else, although whether this someone can be entirely identified with Carrie is not quite certain. The classical analytic inference here would be to say that the person he loves is the mute brother, and it is this bond between men that inhibits Charles from ever tying the knot properly. At the end, it is not just Carrie who is there at the church, it's the brother.

But why the funeral? On an immediate level, it is introduced to contrast with what happens at weddings: the falseness and frivolity of the weddings are checked by the harrowing realities of death, and the veil of vanities is torn aside. But there is more to it than that. The funeral marks the tragic end of a bond between two men, and, as one character points out, they were the only truly happy couple in the whole group. There is thus a contrast not just between weddings and funerals, but between bonds between men and bonds between men and women. What the funeral scene and the moving recital of Auden's verse show is how love is more powerful than the simple empirical presence or absence of the partner. Dead, he can become the focus of an even more powerful love, as the emotional nature of this episode demonstrates. It is immediately after this scene that Charles realises that he has to give up the idea of a perfect match, the one incarnated by two men. And this will be what allows him both to abandon his bride-to-be so heartlessly and to bind himself to Carrie. His barrier is the love relation with his brother, but what the funeral shows is that such a love can endure in the absence of the partner. Lost, he can become a symbol and the focus of a love that lasts.

This is not the only significance of the funeral scene. In folklore, who is it that shows up at weddings? It is not the congregation of families, but the malign influence that much of the wedding ceremony itself is designed to guard against, the evil spirits or ghosts of the dead that return to demand a toll from the living. The vows of marriage are intended more as precautions against these dangers than as a description of the emotions of lovers. Mythology and popular culture are likewise filled with scenes of such spirits returning for a reckoning at the time of a burial or a wake and there is a powerful symmetry between the motif of a parent giving away their child at a wedding and a child giving away their parent at a funeral. In a sense, there is a continuity between this uninvited guest at a funeral and the heterogeneous figure at a wedding, which, in *Four Weddings and a Funeral*, is the American lady with the large hat. It is indeed at her own wedding that the vigorous gay friend dies of heart failure. Thus, rather than taking the cynical view that a wedding is a funeral due to the extinguishing of any individual vitality or because of the break with one's own family, the link is established by the fact that *both suppose an uninvited guest*. When the wedding is transformed into a funeral in *Sleeping Beauty*, it is due precisely to this presence of an uninvited guest, the fairy who casts the spell of deathly sleep on the Princess for having forgotten to invite her to the wedding celebration.

The traditional wedding ritual of the 'false bride' shows how this third party may literally become materialised. Before the vows proper, a false bride is substituted for the real one, and she must be banished before the real bride can take her place. When Carrie makes her first appearance in *Four Weddings*, she steps into a place which folklore has spent many hundreds of years preparing for her: that of the lethal guest. And, as the rest of the story shows, men who spend time around Carrie don't tend to last very long. Might Charles have actually been on the right track with his hesitancy in tying the knot? As she runs through her endless list of past boyfriends, perhaps he could at last find the security that if he got serious with this woman, it wouldn't last very long. And then he could go and repeat the same situation with someone else. Bergler argued that this is in fact one of the main reasons for divorce: if one partner is enjoying the suffering of his relationship too much, he may sacrifice his mate so as to be able to retain the possibility of repeating the same terrible situation with someone else and thus perpetuate his troubles afresh.

Is there a difference here for men and women in their relation to the act of marriage? To Charles' indecisiveness could be matched the great and mysterious abstinence of Queen Elizabeth I. If her father Henry VIII could marry too many times, the daughter would do it too few times. If the story of his life is *Six Weddings and Lots of Funerals*, Elizabeth's destiny becomes *No Weddings and her Own Funeral*. Historians have debated Elizabeth's failure to marry for centuries and they will no doubt continue to do so: was it due to a religious obligation, a state conflict, her own passions or just bad luck? In the famous episode of 1581, she declares in public that she would marry Francis, Duke of Anjou, kisses him on the mouth, gives him a ring and then retracts her promise the next day. Whereas her father cancelled the vows to his first wife that had been in effect for eighteen years, Elizabeth did it overnight. Camden explains this as being due to a temporary imbalance caused by 'the force of modest love in the midst of amorous discourse', from which she is brought to her senses by her councillors and ladies. While the reasons of Elizabeth indeed seem obscure, it is certain that she harboured a particular hostility to the marriage act. Although the marriage of courtiers and ladies in waiting has always been a problem for monarchs, Elizabeth's own reactions to these infidelities were clouded by an unusual venom. On learning of the knot tied between Mary Skelton and James Scudamore, she was intemperate enough to break the lady's finger. This little incident is not unimportant as it can give us a clue to the problem with marriage. After the promise to the Duke of Anjou was retracted, she told him, apparently, that if married she might not long survive the ceremony, an information that suggested to some historians that the idea of marriage and the idea of her mortality were bound together. Given her own unfortunate family history, this would make good sense: after all, her own mother had been executed, and the fate of her father's marriages is well known. The equation of marriage with trouble is thus very plausible. But what about the broken finger? One might recall here that among Elizabeth's troublesome symptoms was a 'gout' in her thumb, a diagnosis which she did not accept, certainly for good reason. And, furthermore, in the time prior to her death, her attendants were curious at her difficulty in removing one of her fingers from her mouth. Other details may be added to this series, which has as its common denominator that there is something wrong with a finger. Now, how does this link to the past, if not via the fact that Elizabeth's mother Anne had a strange appendage, a nascent sixth finger. If the idea of marriage was connected for her to the idea of death, it was through this question of the presence or absence of a finger. Her mother had a part of the body in excess, yet ended her life with a part of the body subtracted. And it is not insignificant that the finger is also the one part of the body which bears the stamp of marriage: the wedding ring. A little thing like a finger thus carries the narrative of generations, and it can tell many stories. Heine once wrote to his beloved sister, 'I utterly bewilder myself every morning by considering whether I would give one or two of my fingers to live a few years by thee', and then, about a decade later, he would watch as two of his fingers became 'crippled', although no certain medical explanation could be found. Many scholars today have turned their talents to writing the histories of such humble objects as the pencil or even rhubarb, and it is not improbable that an 'Illustrated History of the Finger' would both instruct and delight. It may even answer the question of why it is that when men inspect their fingernails they turn the fingers in towards them, whereas woman have the tendency to spread out their hands in front of them.

❦

For men, the problem is not, Should they marry this or that woman? But rather, as Reik pointed out, Should they marry at all? This is a question linked to the law and the place a man has in the symbolic world, which means a relation to one's word. A woman can tell all her friends that she will never get married and yet often secretly harbour a desire to do so, whereas a man can assert the same thing with no comparable wish. And contrary to popular belief, when someone fails to show up at the church, it is most frequently the groom, not the bride-to-be. Whereas for her, the choice not to marry may on occasion be linked to the particularity of the man, the man's choice may be tied less to the specificity of the woman than to his relation to the law as such. He may shrink from the symbolic position that marriage introduces, just as he may do his best to avoid putting a woman in the place of 'wife', as this will evoke the forbidden wife from his childhood: the mother. It is well known that many men can no longer make love to their wives after they become mothers, and if a woman in love can sometimes think of a man as the father of her child, the male lover rarely sees a woman as the mother of his. The place of 'mother' and the place of 'woman' have to be kept as distant as possible, producing from time to time the peculiar idea men have that motherhood and femininity have nothing to do with one another.

If some men thus avoid marriage at all costs, there are nonetheless others who are drawn towards it, not as any kind of expression of their emotions towards the bride than as the result of a duty. This is a capital point. Whereas it is traditionally the woman who is imagined to do so many things out of a grudging sense of obligation (such as make love with the husband), it is frequently the man who is crushed by the weight of debt, and it is a fact that many men make love to women not out of their lust but out of a guilt-ridden sense of duty. They keep on doing things as if a debt has to be paid back, as if something is owed which they pay for, sometimes, with their whole existence. All of their actions become inscribed in a service to the other, even if this other is not physically present. In most cultures, it is religion which produces theories about why we might have such feelings, and which set out the duties of man and the burden he must carry on his shoulders. Being a man, indeed, may mean nothing less than accepting the fact that one owes something, and Christianity has its own versions of what this signifies. We may have a debt to pay due to what happened in the Garden of Eden, whether we like it or not, or, in another version, due to what we have done in our own lives: we sin either *because* Adam did, or *as* Adam did. Love life thus carries a shadow from the past, which may bring with it its own limits. But what happens when people try to escape this, to shed the bonds of obligation and release themselves from the mechanisms of debt? The paradox here is that the commonest version of such a release involves a contract even more binding, even more absolute and inescapable than the first, a contract not with the Deity but with Satan. People who make contracts with the Devil ought to know that whatever favours they can conjure will not last. And yet, like lovers, their urgency of purpose is never matched by an alertness to the future.

Three

It is strange that contracts which involve speaking are usually associated in some way with the Deity, whereas to make a contract with the Devil, speech isn't enough. What he wants is a contract in writing, even in one's own blood. But why should speech suffice for a god or for lovers, but not for a devil? It has been argued, in fact, that the gods actually owe their existence to our promises: if they didn't exist, we wouldn't be able to swear by them. Hence Callimachus was much amused on reading a biblical passage in which God swears in his own name. But if so many promises are made in the name of another, it might be objected that we in fact give more than speech to a deity: if the Devil gets blood, another part of the body is given in ritual mutilations or in circumcision. So many initiation ceremonies revolve around the extraction or marking of a part of the body, be it a tooth or a finger or a toe. But in each case, a contract is secured on parting with a little bit of flesh.

Christianity has distanced itself from such practices with its avoidance of changes to the flesh, even if it continues to prescribe garments, hairstyle and the application of water in baptism. The real difference between the divine and the satanic contract would consist in the fact that if the Devil demands a bit of the body, this bit of the body is used to *write with*. And, just as many people think that it is easier to shake off the bonds of a spoken contract like marriage, the leasing of oneself to the Devil has a kind of absolute character. Whatever happens, there's no getting out of it.

But why is this motif of debt so powerful and why is there such an air of certainty to it?

Although Freud quotes the *Faust* of Goethe innumerable times, it is quite baffling why he never devoted a paper to the Faust story itself, despite the dignity of this myth alongside that of Oedipus. In 1922 he did write an account of a seventeenth-century case of supposed demoniacal possession, but even though the collaborator who published simultaneously his own perspective on the events which took place in the town of Mariazell chose to entitle his paper 'Faust in Mariazell', Freud strangely avoids bringing in the Faust story. Haizmann, a young painter, has given his bond to the Devil in writing and now, when the term of the accord is almost up, he seeks the intervention of the Blessed Virgin to save him. Salvation will take the precise form here of giving up a bit of paper, the return of the bond which had been drafted in his own blood. Things work out and Haizmann gets the bond back, but a further bout of convulsive illness leads him back to Mariazell. Now, he says, he must obtain an earlier bond, drafted in ink. Again, he obtains it, and soon joins an order of monks.

What interests Freud in all this is the motive of the bond with the Devil. Usually, the Devil can offer something to the one who has leased his soul, be it wisdom or the enjoyment of beautiful women, but in this case there is no mention of any material return. Hence Freud's question: what did the painter want? Examining the wording of the contracts, he argues that in the absence of any mention of an undertaking, he is giving up his soul not for something to be obtained from the Devil but for something the Devil must in fact *do* for him. It would seem, then, that the object of the painter's desire is the demand of the other: rather than seeing the contract as the condition of some access to an object, the contract is the object itself.

Rather than developing this interesting implication, Freud argues that there is indeed a concealed service here, suggested by the reference to what he assumes is the recent death of the painter's father. The contract thus renders the service of a replacement: the Devil undertakes to stand in for the man's father for the term of nine years. Which leads Freud to a discussion of the son's relation to the father, the axis of which is the ambivalence of love and hate. Just as the father has two sides to him, the loving and the terrifying, so the original deity had all the terrifying features that would later be combined to form the image of his satanic counterpart. From this discussion, Freud turns to the question of the bonds, and explains the oddity of the existence of the second bond in terms of the painter's justifications to the religious figures of Mariazell: if he became delirious once more, that would imply that the return of the first bond had not worked, and therefore the introduction of the second. This might explain the circumstance, but it equally suggests another conclusion: the second bond is necessary since, once the first is returned, there still has to be a contract. However many bits of paper are sent back, there is always one which is out of reach, yet binding. When we look through contracts today we are alert to the small print, but in the story it is not a contingent feature of the bond but its essence. For the painter, the small print takes the form of the first contract itself. Freud's avoidance of a discussion of the Faust story is even odder here, given the fact that he draws attention to the drafting of the contracts in both blood and ink. As is well known, according to a certain myth the original Faust had himself been a printer, and his overnight production of numerous Bibles printed in a red ink fired suspicions that he must have conjured them up by sorcery. The red ink was blood, and a pact with the Devil was thus most reasonably supposed: and so Faust was born, according to this version of events. The continuum of ink and blood is echoed in the Haizmann narrative, which allows one to come closer to the heart of the mystery of the terrible agreement.

If we generalise to account for the popularity of the legend of Faust and take seriously the attention to writing, it may be concluded that Faust makes his contract not with Satan but with a Printer, or, more precisely, with a printing press. The demon to which he gives up body and soul is the demon of language. When one of the most popular sixteenth-century Faustbooks summed up its narrative, the whole story became condensed as 'his writing, his promise, and end'. It all starts with a piece of writing, with language, and his fate is linked to this commitment. The contract is with the order of language, which is why however many contracts you get rid of, there will always be one left. And a contract, after all, may seem like a promise, but it involves much more: it is there to guarantee that one's words will be binding, that language will have certain effects that one cannot get out of. This is indeed the contract that separates adults from children: as Lacan pointed out, the difference is in the binding qualities of the word. For adults, the word commits you, but a child can say as many charming or insulting things as it likes without being arrested. Age seems to defer the mantle of commitment, although today this is becoming a more complex legal topic, when the words of children have to be assessed in new contexts in which questions of truth and falsity become paramount.

At what moment, then, does one become committed to the word? The reason that Faust is a myth is because this moment is not a real, empirical one but a logical time. There is not one date after which what the child says is binding. It is something that has to take place, but we can't situate it, just like growing taller: the Faust story exists, perhaps, because of this difficulty. As Lacan argued, when something seems impossible to formulate or think through in the usual way, it can take on the form of a myth. It presents a narrative of the debt incurred on entering the world of language. But why should this all be so devilish? Doesn't entering the symbolic world bring with it a sort of pacification or temperance, leaving behind the storms of infancy? Once again, this is where the Faust story illustrates what is really involved in this transformation: the symbolic world might be pacifying and it might embody the network of the law, but there will always be something discordant at its heart, terrifying and demanding, forever unsatisfied and bent on destruction. This is what Freud called the superego, an agency which internalises in the psyche the imperatives of one's parents, setting out limits and telling you what is forbidden. In this first formulation it's like the angel in comic books battling with the devilish figure who tempts the character to err. But as Freud details the model of the superego, it emerges as more complex, even contradictory. This is because it does not just incarnate what the parent tells you not to do but also what you have to do but are not allowed to: it pushes its host to be like the one who escapes the prohibitions in question.

Freud's students did the logical thing and separated the angelic and devilish aspects, calling them the ideal and the superego respectively, the latter term describing the voice that compels you, for example, to sleep with the woman that the ideal tells you not to sleep with. The Freudian idea is that the more you renounce, the more you follow the angel and become a good citizen, the more the superego will be feeding off the satisfactions you have given up. The better you are, the more your superego will ravage you, generating unhappiness and painful symptoms. The difference from the comic book model is that in this strange but very accurate conception, the more successful the angel is, the more powerful the devil becomes. The more you give up to the angel, the more there is for the devil to consume. The satanic figure in Faust who demands his repayment embodies this dreadful force, materialised whenever the contract with the symbolic has been set. The more that satisfaction is renounced in becoming a model little boy or girl, the more it will take on a consistency somewhere else, complicating the usual separation of saints and sinners and confirming the Church's definition of a saint: someone who has been under-researched.

So what is the Faust story all about? A man sells his soul to the Devil in exchange for a certain number of years in which he may profit from unusual powers and privileges. At the end of this term, he will regret his action, and desperately try to cancel the debt, but it is something which cannot be revoked, and he is taken. It is a story about debt, but with a particular emphasis. Faust will enjoy many years of his life with the powers granted him, and therefore the debt he owes at the end is a debt for nothing less than his existence. To be, for Faust, involves the presence of something owed. If the story of Oedipus is the story of someone who has a desire to know, the story of Faust, as one scholar points out, is of someone who has a desire to be. He is less concerned with knowing more than other men, than being more than other men. What one religious perspective could add here is that for this debt to be set in place, it is not a contract with a real devil that is necessary, but perhaps nothing more than the fact of one's own birth.

If Freud did not turn his attentions to the Faust story as such, he did author some peculiar lines about the idea of a debt of birth. The clinical phenomenon which he is trying to explain is the fact that many men have the compulsion to rescue a woman. Marcel Pagnol tells us that even before his baccalaureate, he had, in his daydreams, rescued at least a dozen different women, saving them from cruel kidnappers, raging storms, volcanic eruptions and even earthquakes. The rescue fantasy is a common one, and Freud is trying to explain its frequency. He has argued earlier on in his papers on the psychology of love that the man's choice of mate will follow from the vicissitudes of his relation with his mother. Denying the sexual side of the latter, the man will split his object into the idealised lady, with whom he cannot sleep, and the degraded sexual being, with whom he can. The splitting in the man's love life is thus a consequence of his failure to confront the sexual side of the mother, the fact that she, like other women, can make love and may even enjoy it. When a man has the urge to rescue a woman he loves, it may seem to follow from this: he will choose a sexual creature, for example a prostitute, and endeavour to remove her from her surroundings and the confining characteristics of her life. The sexual would thus be shifted over to the idealised. Charles Dickens devoted much energy to his attempts to rescue fallen women, but, as the critic Claire Tomalin points out, despite meeting so many of them, the image of the fallen woman in his writing is always the same. Following the first part of the Freudian argument, this is no surprise: the image is the same because it refers to the same woman, the mother, refracted through the features of the many women to whom he would offer his good works.

But Freud is not convinced by this part of the argument: the impulse to rescue, he thinks, is 'an independent derivative' of what he calls the 'parental complex'. It is thus not simply linked to the image of the mother. The idea would be that as the child learns that it owes its life to its parents, his feelings of tenderness unite with impulses which aim at power and independence and the wish to return the gift emerges. As Freud formulates it, the child's defiance takes the form: 'I want nothing from my father: I will give him back all I have cost him.' And hence the fantasy of rescuing the father from danger and saving his life. This fantasy will then be displaced to a king or well-known person, as may be seen in many literary creations. This view would seem to be supported by the curious fact that when someone rescues someone else and the debt is paid, so often it is the life of an enemy that is in question. The one who owes you his life is in fact originally a rival, which would make sense given Freud's argument that the one who is saved is a representative of the father. But the symmetry is complicated by the fact that it is not so easy, Freud thinks, to pay back the mother: it will take the form of either giving her a child or making a child for her. The idea of rescuing the father has its roots in defiance, whereas the gift to the mother is linked more closely with tender feelings. The child offered to her will no doubt resemble the son himself, and thus the son will turn into his own father. It is as if the Sabellian heresy that the Son is Himself his own father is articulated in each set of these fantasies of rescue.

But is the idea of rescue identical for both man and woman? Do they both aim, in the rescue fantasy, at the same thing? Freud's response to this question is negative. Rescuing can mean, for a man, producing a child, in the sense of causing it to be born, and in a woman, to give birth to a child herself. Interesting as they may be, these explanations do not exhaust the motif of rescue. Freud would acknowledge this, encouraging his students to write a paper with the title 'Motives of Rescue and Redemption in Fantasy and Neurosis', and a footnote he added to his book on the psychopathology of everyday life puts in question the earlier explanation of the meaning of rescue for the man. In a discussion of daydreams, he had evoked the episode in Daudet's 'Le Nabab' in which a Monsieur Jocelyn throws himself at the head of a runaway horse in a Paris street, bringing it to a halt. Out steps a great personage, takes Jocelyn's hand and says, 'You are my saviour. I owe my life to you. What can I do for you?' But as Freud checks his sources just before going to press, he finds that this story is not to be found in Daudet. And there is no Monsieur Jocelyn either, only a Monsieur Joyeuse, a name which contains a form of Freud's own name translated into French. The daydream, he concludes, must be his own, perhaps thought up on one of his lonely walks in Paris as a young man, searching for a protector and patron. Freud continues to point out that he has always felt antagonistic to the idea of being someone's protégé, feeling instead the urge to be 'the strong man' himself. The daydream would thus make sense on Freud's rescue model where a debt is paid back as an act of defiance. But in a footnote added in 1924, he now discusses a possible source of the story in a children's book, and writes that the rescue phantasy of the great man was merely elaborated as a prelude to the fantasy of *his own rescue* by the latter. At the conscious level, he is resistant to being dependent on anyone else, yet at a more profound level, it is the other man who saves him and gives him his prize.

This pattern is indeed present in many of the rescue daydreams that we hear about in psychoanalysis, but a word of caution ought to be added here about their interpretation. It might seem that a daydream is a wish, that it represents what we really want, but the fact is that the romances of love and rescue do not indicate what the daydreamer is really after: to find that out, it is better to look not at the daydream but at the day. The situations of misery that many people construct for themselves testify to their more profound aims, the daydreams being a sort of cover, although, as the Freud example showed, the clues can be found here to access the deeper material. Thus it is interesting to follow a daydream to find other material, but it would be a mistake to identify it with the answer to the question of what a person wants.

A man described a series of daydreams he had entertained in his early adolescence, in which he rescued another schoolboy, the son of eminent parents, from a gang of cut-throats. The image of this other boy was detailed in such a way to make it clear that he embodied, in part, certain traits which his father had privileged as ideal. Once the rescue had taken place, the daydreamer was rewarded lavishly by this boy's family. The form of the reward, a sum of money, was linked to what the father situated as beyond himself, the profits he forever dreamt of yet never accrued. The son thus received, in the daydream, what he had not received from his father, and the rescue took on its place as a part of a more complicated structure which involved less the son's act of defiance than a new form of indebtedness. When Robert Browning entertained a little fantasy about rescuing Elizabeth Barrett from robbers and having her hand bestowed on him in gratitude, it might seem that what is involved here is simply a wish, to have the hand of the woman. But the crucial feature is the fact that he doesn't just have access to the woman: she is *bestowed*.

If the only concern was to access a forbidden woman, people would have fantasies about stealing women rather than about rescuing them. Which some people certainly do. If she is bestowed, however, we are closer to the oedipal idea that if the mother is renounced, another woman will be promised for the future, sanctioned by the father. Browning dreamt about rescue in this sense, since the woman could then be received from someone else, as a gift, a recompense: in other words, in legitimacy. Analysing a wide range of folk tales and myths, the Russian philologist Vladimir Propp enumerated a set of familiar characters – the villain, the princess and so on – yet he added the figure of the donor, which takes on a sense here in terms of the function of bestowing. But what exactly is the nature of this function?

If Freud's Nabab story shows that rescue *of* the father can translate into rescue *by* the father, we have to ask the question of what sort of father is doing the rescuing. In the early years of psychoanalysis, there was once a debate about the universality of the Oedipus complex and scholars devoted much energy to combing reports of indigenous cultures to look for evidence. In his deep and varied studies, Ernest Jones became curious as to why it was that in many such cultures, pregnancy was linked less to the real penis than to the presence of some sort of spirit, what he called an 'idea'. Rather than attributing this apparently strange belief to simple ignorance, he argued that as a child is caught in the turbulence of the Oedipus complex, with its hostile wishes and anxieties focusing on the father, he will do the best possible thing: separate the mother from the real father by making of a spirit the cause of her pregnancy rather than the man who's close to home. The introduction of the symbolic element, the idea, thus has a mediating effect and introduces a pacification of the terrible oedipal situation. And hence the birth, in analytic doctrine, of more than one father: to the man with a real penis is added the figure of the symbolic, intangible one. The Church, of course, has had its own engagements with this problem, as seen in the debates over the exact relations of Father, Son and Holy Ghost. It is not a real man who lies behind the birth of the baby Jesus, but an agency or spirit which is separate from the reality of the father himself. It was thus perfectly logical for so-called heretics like Origen and Arius to insist on qualifying the metaphors of paternity to avoid the idea of a physical emission of some substance in the works of the Deity. Although it was argued at the time that the idea of some emission would suggest unacceptably that God was divisible and changeable, the latent polemic is against the proximity of a real father who emits sperm, and a symbolic one, who doesn't. And if God did emit in this way, the 'Let there be light' of the creation would suggest, equally unacceptably, that the world is the result of a nocturnal emission.

In psychoanalytic theory, it was Lacan who developed these ideas about the symbolic side of paternity, differentiated from the real biological function of the father, and in many cases we can see that in the scenario of rescue it is this function that is ultimately appealed to. When the image of the real father is for some reason crippled, a symbolic element can come to reinforce it, in the same way that a coat of arms can give a family stature regardless of the state of its dissolution. In the first volume of Marcel Pagnol's autobiography there is a beautiful example of the use of a symbolic element to reinforce the weakened image of the father. The young Marcel is a great admirer of his schoolteacher father, yet when his Aunt Rose takes up with the wealthier and more polished gentleman Jules, the paternal image is quietly undermined. The two families rent a holiday villa together, and the men go off shooting: whereas Marcel's father had never killed beast or bird before, Jules is, of course, an expert. His gun is magnificent, whereas the father's is out of date and rather absurd. As Marcel watches the sizing up of the two guns, he feels humiliated, and a strange malaise sets in, a vague dissatisfaction, the cause of which he does not understand. When he does realise what is going on, the problem is not removed: his father, the great teacher, has now become the schoolboy, instructed by Uncle Jules, the specialist. For the first time, Marcel says, he doubts the 'omnipotence' of his father.

As the two men continue to hunt, the field of their trophies is divided neatly into two parts, the animals that they can and do hit like the ordinary partridge, rabbit or hare, and one special animal which is distinguished from all the others, which has a separate privileged place: the rock partridge. This is the ultimate prize of the hunter, yet its value is matched by its rarity. As little Marcel assists the adults on their hunt, he does his best to restore the crippled image of the father: he produces some feathers, at one moment, to persuade Jules that his father had hit something. Banned from trailing along on their hunt, he follows in secret, abject at his father's generally poor show compared with Jules'. Until suddenly the father strikes it lucky: he shoots not just one rock partridge, which would have been miracle enough, but two, one of them landing on the son's head. While Jules admonishes Marcel's father for having missed the rare birds, Marcel emerges from the undergrowth carrying these trophies. As they visit town to show off their work, the local inhabitants are struck dumb by this unheard of feat, and the father is photographed proud and dignified. Later, he will send a copy of the photograph to his own father, thus giving the rock partridges a value in the link between generations. And it is now that Marcel feels a great love for his father . . .

This story, finely told in Pagnol's book *My Father's Glory*, illuminates the function of the symbolic element in the context of the child's oedipal narrative. The father is idealised, until the arrival of Uncle Jules whose gun is better. The father is progressively humiliated, until the splendid hunting episode, where he takes on his crest, in the form of the rock partridges. They function exactly as a coat of arms, fixing not only transgenerational identity – the photo sent to the grandfather – but also conferring nobility on their bearer. The birds have had a special value since the start of the story, distinguished from other animals, as a mythic bounty: they are not simply real birds, *they are symbols*.

And as one of these symbols falls on to the head of the boy, the father's glory crowns the son. The symbolic elements thus bolster the weakened image of the father, and the son can continue his saga to do the next logical thing in the second volume of the memoir, which is to pass through the romance with the mother.

Beyond the many images of the rescue fantasy, we thus find the appeal to the symbolic, the rescuing function which is distinct from a real human being. This would also explain a curious remark Freud makes in his first unpublished version of the article dealing with rescue. He says that the motif is linked to the idea of finding a woman who will save the child from masturbation, someone who will put an end to the forbidden activity. Although this point is not included in the published version, it shows that the idea of rescue may be connected to the idea of an agency of prohibition, exactly the agency that is incarnated by the symbolic elements we have discussed. What rescues is never ultimately human, and the heraldic rock partridges of Pagnol may be linked in a series to the robot of *Terminator 2* which is there to remove the future saviour of mankind from danger. That this symbolic element must be distinguished from what is human is clear from the Lassie stories: once again, it is an animal that comes to the rescue, and indeed, whether it be a dog or a dolphin, what animals do in television series is always the same: they save people.

If we compare the Faust story and the rescue motif, a tension emerges between the idea of cancelling a debt and the idea that a debt can never be cancelled. If a figure like Gandhi could devote his whole life to saving others, it is significant that he resolves to do so after he leaves his ailing father to go and hurriedly make love to his wife. Their embraces were interrupted by a knock on the door and a servant tells him that in that short space of time away from the sickbed, his father has died. This debt to the father which can never be repaid thus becomes the determination to rescue everyone else, the crusade which would make up the rest of Gandhi's life. In a sense, the rescue fantasy here may be seen as generated by the Faustian impossibility: the daydream is of repaying, but it is a daydream precisely because the debt can never be repaid in full.

We need to examine in more detail the different possibilities and versions of these motifs. When Freud's student Karl Abraham examined the theme of rescue, he had the idea that it may conceal not simply a defiance of the father, but the urge to murder him and block his sexual commerce with the mother. But is the image of rescuing the mother simply an expression of the wish to give her a child? The detail with which Freud begins his discussion of rescue fantasies is an important one: the woman rescued is often of loose morals. She belongs, in a sense, to other men. Since the mother is a woman who belongs to another man (the father), the derivation of rescue from the oedipal constellation would seem obvious. Hence we should be all the more surprised that when Freud is studying exactly this pattern, the first example he gives is not of rescuing the mother, but the father. Rescuing him pays him back and thus puts him, for the son, out of the picture. This would suggest that rescue fantasies follow a logical development, starting with rescue of the father, followed by that of the mother, but, as we have seen, Freud's discussion of the Daudet story makes things not quite as they seem. The rescue *of* the father covers over a rescue *by* the father, or, more precisely, by a symbolic element which is differentiated from the real father. The problem that is introduced by these motifs is crucial: what it means for a man to receive something.

❦

There are many men who are incapable of either giving or receiving, although it is rare to find an inability to receive and an inability to give in one and the same person: it is generally either the one or the other. And where some men reject everything that is offered by their father with scorn, turning instead to the mother, others can never, on any condition, accept anything from the mother. Whatever the parent gives them, it isn't right, be it an article of clothing or an instruction in some skill. There will always be something that doesn't fit. And yet these men who have a problem with receiving will be the same men who give a lot, particularly to the opposite sex. It is a fact that the more altruistic a man is, especially in the act of sex itself, the more likely it is his feelings will settle into hate. If a woman takes on the value for a man of the one who must be satisfied at all costs, this investiture will cause no small number of problems later on. If he can't satisfy her, his hatred will spark, and if he thinks he can satisfy her, she will become the object of an equal antipathy, as embodying the enjoyment he is himself separated from. The more a man tries to give to a woman, the more he will end up hating her.

Similarly, there are men who are quite happy to take a lot of things from other people, yet are fundamentally unable to really give anything themselves, as we see in the fact that the people who are completely incapable of ever being alone are in fact the same people who are incapable of ever really being with other people. Taking a lot here does not mean having a lot. Many men dream about making money, but when they finally have some success, they make sure that their earnings disappear, to complain afterwards that they just don't know what happened: the determination here is to keep the pockets empty at all costs, and probably to make sure that it is someone else who is imagined to have what they've lost. When Heine was awarded his degree in law, he received a relatively large sum of money from his millionaire uncle Solomon to be spent on a well-deserved holiday. Yet the moment he reached the island of Nordeney, he gambled it away so recklessly that all was lost in one night. For this man, it was imperative to get something, yet whatever he had, he would lose. Heine would spend his whole life in search of the sum of money from his wealthy relatives that would put an end to his miseries. He lived with this vision of the future, despite sabotaging any chances he might have had by his celebrated insolence and disobedience to Uncle Solomon.

English culture has its own version of this economic balance. When Nick Leeson brought down Baring's bank in 1995, the big mystery was not, Why did the senior bankers let themselves be fooled for so long? But rather, Why was Leeson always grinning after his arrest? The trader requested funds from the bank to cover initial payments for clients who had no existence except on Leeson's account sheets in order to cover his growing losses. Finally, with no hope of saving himself after the fall of the market, he escapes with his wife for a brief holiday before flying to Frankfurt where he is arrested. As he is led away by the waiting officials, he is trying hard to hold back his grin. In the publicity of the following months, he is unable to do even that. But why is someone who lost so much so pleased?

It might appear that the grin is simply a sign of relief: under enormous pressure for so long, the trader now no longer has anything to hide. He can admit to the banking disasters and accept his deserts. But something more profound is at work here, there is a glee which is not merely the effect of catharsis: this man was in a lot of trouble and yet he was clearly very pleased about something. Leeson's grin can be put into a series with Dreyfus' sleep. As his life collapsed around him and he was brought to a heinous trial, the French soldier was sleeping like a baby. Presumably at some level, the punishment carried with it a satisfaction, even if the person in question was not actually guilty of the crime. In the early days of psychoanalysis, an enthusiastic judge offered those convicted of the sexual perversion of exhibitionism the chance to avoid prison if they undertook treatment at the Vienna Psychoanalytic Clinic. He would pass a suspended sentence and remit their punishment if they could demonstrate after six months that they were in analytic treatment. At first, five cases were referred, to be treated free of charge. The first man gave up a few days after receiving the written confirmation that he had begun treatment. The next two didn't show up after their first interview with the clinic's director, and the others withdrew with the weakest of excuses. It was not the treatment itself they were so afraid of, since they had no idea of what it would be like, they had seen different practitioners and they did not even know each other. Rather, they all chose imprisonment as the punishment as a part of their psychic rhythm: prison was not just a contingent consequence of a lawless action but a part of the movement between crime and punishment. As one of the analysts concluded, without imprisonment, they would not have had the ticket permitting their next crime to take place. The guilt and the crime are thus in a peculiar yet logical relationship. Leeson, perhaps, was grinning because he had found what he was searching for.

The neurotic relation to receiving is played out in spectacular form in this case. Leeson is inventing imaginary clients to buy futures and then ends up buying them back himself. As the debt grows bigger, his profits appear to grow, and the bank sends vast sums of money to cover him. In other words, not only was Leeson concerned with the image he displayed to the bank, anxious that they still saw him as a wonder boy, but he was spending what he did not have. He was obtaining money by deception, which only fell into the bottomless pit of his ever accruing debt. The profits he was making, as he admitted afterwards, 'were not true profits', and it is this question of what a true profit is which gives the key to understanding what is perhaps the central difficulty of masculinity. Having something, yet something which exists in the form of a promise: a profit, but not a true one. The masculine position could in fact be defined as the acceptance that there is no such thing as a true profit. Thus the often comic oscillation of men between strength and dependency ceases to be a contradiction. The two qualities are not contradictory since strength, for a man, is always *borrowed*. It is surely no accident that superheroes are not superheroes all the time: they are regular guys until they suddenly transform into superheroes – and then they change back. Like Asterix, their special powers are transitory, not permanent, on loan, not inherent. Goethe could write that what man inherits from his forefathers has to be earned to be possessed, but such possession is never complete. It means that when the man has something, it doesn't really belong to him.

When the financial market was sent spinning by the bursting of the South Sea Bubble, a physician specialising in nervous disorders made the observation that although he now had a huge number of new patients, they were not the ones who had lost everything but, on the contrary, those who had sold their stock just in time. It was this dimension of the narrow escape, the possibility rather than the reality of losing something, that was so difficult to bear, demonstrating the real difficulties of having. Even at the peak of his success, the actor Spencer Tracy would lie awake at night trying to calculate how much he and his wife would need to live on if his career collapsed. With each success, he would be plagued by the thought that he'd somehow fooled the public and that someday they would 'catch on to him' and he would lose everything. When Lacan said that the boy must have the phallus but the phallus is a signifier, he illuminated exactly these difficulties. What does it mean to have something which is a signifier? It is clearly not the same as having some tangible object, such as a penis or a car. One could in fact define the masculine impasse here as strictly equivalent to the difficulty one might have in understanding Lacan's sentence. A man's problem in understanding what it might mean to 'have a signifier' is identical with man's problem, and it leads him into all sorts of difficulties.

After a short period of treatment, a man developed a peculiar fear. Whenever he was getting into his bath, he would have the panicky feeling that he was still wearing his watch, which was not waterproof. The value of the possession became linked with the possibility of its being damaged, showing how having for a man is never a simple thing. It could be pointed out that whereas a woman sometimes forgets where she has parked, it is much more common for a man to have the terrible fear that when he gets back to his car, it just won't be there. The general problem of having becomes articulated in the whole series of his possessions, particularly those which are linked with the idea of the masculine trait. The penis, of course, has its privileged place in this series, and although most men don't consciously go around worrying about losing it, it is a fact that when a man finds a trace of blood in his urine or some other irregularity linked to the genitals, he will experience an uncanny feeling, in contrast with the greater equanimity with which a woman can observe the same symptoms.

Bergler had his own idea about the problems of receiving. In an endless series of books and articles, he argued that the wish to take seems obvious to everyone, shrink or not shrink, yet it is only a description, and a deceptive one at that. Beneath it is the real impulse, not to take but to be refused, so strong that it generates its own schedule: first of all, an external situation will be misused in such a way that disappointment and refusal are produced. The world is thus identified with what Bergler calls the 'refusing mother'. Then, phase two, not really aware of the fact that they have brought this refusal on themselves, they fight back, to give the pseudo-aggressive appearance of the neurotic. And finally, beaten, they indulge in self-pity, unconsciously enjoying their misery, and bemoaning that 'This can only happen to me'. Rather than accepting what Bergler calls their masochism, they continue their lives feeling like martyrs, no doubt because it is more pleasant to think of oneself as a martyr than as a masochist. Now, as a description of a pattern that many people introduce into their lives and indeed use as a sort of personal organiser, none of this is false. The problems are rather in Bergler's explanation of why there is this desire to be refused in the first place.

The pain and fury of the growing child are not tolerable for long, says Bergler, without some libidinalisation of the blows he daily receives. The only solution to the disappointment, humiliation and despair he experiences is to coat them with the sugar of his libido, and turn the spears of his fury into boomerangs. The time gap between crying and feeding is only one of the miseries to be endured, to which are added the great terrors of childhood: fear of starvation, fear of being poisoned, fear of being choked, fear of being chopped to pieces, fear of being drained and the fear of castration. If the reader is amazed that such fears exist and has no memory of them, remember that they are unconscious and will emerge regardless of the actual parenting that the child receives. They represent a basic set of terrors that, if veiled in their expression in early life, often emerge with clarity not in childhood but in old age, where they may in fact be a cause of death (refusal to eat due to fear of poisoning etc.). How else might one explain the success of the modest and unassuming film *Misery*, in which a disturbed fan holds as prisoner an author whom she has abducted. For most of the film, the captive is bed-ridden, completely at the mercy of this woman who feeds him, cares for him, and watches over him. The fascination is in this helplessness: he might be desperate to escape, but he cannot even physically outwit his captor due to a leg injury. A grown man is thus exactly in the situation of a child at the mercy of his mother, and if childhood is generally depicted in our culture as some kind of paradise, *Misery* gives perhaps the best picture available of what it is really like at a certain level of the psyche. People can't remember this, of course, due to repression, but the power of the film can give them a clue, as can the anger men so often feel when they are having their heads moved for them at the barber shop.

The problem here, which has divided psychoanalytic authors for so long, is to choose between interpreting the malevolence of the captor as either the real menace of the caregiver or simply as the reflected form of the captive's own anger at frustrations, a theme to which we shall return later on. It is worth noting here the way in which a specific disappointment or frustration for a child does not produce the response, 'You are really very nice but in this particular case I did not appreciate your behaviour', but is generalised from the detail into a broader feeling of hatred. What matters here are the unusual, inconsistent and unexpected reactions of the parent, a fact which can explain the puzzle frequently discussed by those investigating the language of children. Rather than expecting to find a match, for example, between the frequency of a grammatical form used by the parent and its emergence in the child's speech, it is the form which doesn't fit, which may have only been used once, which may take on a special value due precisely to its irregularity.

Now, to return to the list of infantile terrors, Bergler thinks that they will be searched for rather than avoided, to give the 'psychic masochism' that he was so keen to expound. The interest of this conception is that at least it explains, in part, why there should be an unconscious enjoyment in what is consciously experienced as suffering. To describe self-destructive behaviour as 'self-destructive behaviour' without any further details doesn't explain anything, supposing the very thing that has to be accounted for, just as explaining things in terms of a traumatic experience in the past is not especially helpful either. If a man has had a cruel and vicious mother in his childhood, he may well perpetuate the same situation later on in life with his spouse, but equally he may choose a tender and loving wife. Freud said something very interesting here in a letter to Abraham. A childhood trauma, he wrote, does not cause a neurosis, but may be responsible for the *form* of its symptoms. Thus tracing the form of a symptom – for example, the choice of a tormenting and abusive spouse – to a moment of torment and abuse in childhood is not enough: what needs to be added is the framework in which this transposition has taken place. Why was the situation perpetuated and into what logic was it inserted? To take our example from *Brief Encounter* once again, it may turn out that Alec had been involved in some painful childhood scene involving the extraction of a piece of grit from someone's eye, but how this detail became lodged in his own phantasy, the framework of his own making, is another question.

Interpreting Freud's paper 'On Female Sexuality', Bergler continued to argue how the oedipal situation is produced from these early anxieties. Freud suspected that seeing in the one person of the mother a giving and refusing, loving and hating and loved and hated being leads the child, if male, to invest the father with the hatred originally directed to the mother, thus dividing hostile and tender currents. If female, the child will invert the split, and it is the father who receives the tender currents. This leads to the oedipal stage proper, in which, for Bergler, its true function as a rescue station emerges. Helpless and victimised by the terrifying mother, the child tries one last manoeuvre: he demotes her to an image of his own passive, victimised self, elevating the father into the position of power, so that it now appears that the mother is entirely under the father's dominion. By identifying with the father, the child can then reassure himself and place his libidinal wishes. Again, the interest of Bergler's idea is that it responds to the clinical fact that, at a certain age, children do begin to elevate one of their parents, even if nothing in the family situation seems to warrant it. The most subdued and bullied husband suddenly becomes the vanquisher of the mother, and it is this sort of occurrence that Bergler's ideas are responding to. The father is now in the position of rescuer, even if this accomplishment is based on the child's last desperate bid to escape from the mother and his powers are thus illusory. The rescuer, following this argument, will always be the father, but is this really the case? The main problem with this sort of argument is that it entirely neglects the functioning of symbolic structures. As we saw from the discussion of rescue, what is appealed to in many instances is a symbolic element, distinct from the reality of the parent. The question, however, which still remains unexplored, is the theme of rescue as it is different for boys and girls.

A woman's ideas of rescue may be immediately distinguished from those of a man. If a man often wants to remove a woman from her apparently dissolute life, it is to make her his own property and situate her within the confines of the routines he has established himself. Hence the well-known motif of the man who rescues a prostitute to make her his obedient wife. Gladstone might not have married one, but his passion for saving ladies of the night was so strong that he would feel a strange emptiness in his life whenever he stopped. What he wanted was something far worse than a sexual commerce: as he read Tennyson for four-hour stints to his dissipated listeners, his goal was nothing less than a real change in their existence, a substitution of his horrifyingly moral agenda for their own. In contrast, a woman may aim less to turn a living man into a mortified one, than to accomplish an inverse operation: to take a man who seems mortified – for example, a man in jail – and make him come alive.

A young woman continues an unhappy affair with an unhappily married man. Each time he lets her down, she has the thought that things will be different next time, until, one morning, she wakes up and stares at a photograph she had placed by her bed of a woman walking on a beach holding a hand, the body of which cannot be seen. And at that moment the formula of her relation to the man appears: she wants to 'raise him from the dead'. If many men want to rescue women from life to make them dead, this woman aimed, on the contrary, at rescuing a man from the dead to make him alive. If the princess kisses the frog to make him her prince, a man is more likely to kiss a frog to make it his manageable property. If the frog gets a bit bigger and becomes a beast, he may, as in some versions of the story, turn into an ideal man, or, in a male version, the beautiful woman may suddenly turn into a beast, as in the film *Species* in which an alien monster periodically emerges out of its 'container', the body of a ravishing woman, to eliminate various men. There are some people who hold the belief that, in a past life, they actually were one of these creatures. If one enquires for evidence, a host of dreams may be produced which all feature a certain animal. But rather than proving that the dreamer was a frog in their past life, what such dreams demonstrate, if anything, is that in a past life they were someone who was looking at a frog. The dream, after all, is not dreamt from a frog's eye view. If such convictions have their interest, it is rather in the idea, central to a current of feminine sexuality, of rebirth and resurrection.

As the young Rebecca West is digging up specially buried conkers, her father asks her what she's up to. 'I am God,' she replies, 'and they are people, and I made them die and now I am resurrecting them.' Her father was curious. 'Why did you make the people die,' he said, 'if you meant to dig them up again?' To which Rebecca replies, 'Well, that would have been all right for them. But it would have been no fun for me.' Fun can conceal a logic, and we find the same motif of something coming back to life in her first book, *The Return of the Soldier*. This short novel begins with the introduction of the couple Chris and Kitty, who have lost their son Oliver. Chris returns from the war suffering from shell-shock and is unable to recognise his wife, only his previous love Mrs Grey. Kitty does her best to make him remember, showing him the rings and necklaces he had given her. As his passion for Mrs Grey continues, the women wonder about how to bring him back, to make this soldier return in the sense of returning to his wife. Mrs Grey has the idea that he should be reminded of his dead son, but once the jersey and ball of the latter are in her hands, she refuses to take them out to the soldier, claiming instead that the idea was simply her way of getting closer to the lost boy. Leave him, she says, as he is, but reconsidering, she goes down to give the objects to him, an action that is implied rather than explicitly described, as with the supposed 'cure' of the soldier at the end. If conkers are important here, it is in the ambiguity of the 'return': on one level, it is the return from the battlefront of the soldier, but it is also the return to his former love, the return from his amnesia to his wife Kitty and the return of the memory of the son. It is something dug up which brings the soldier back to his life, although the book also suggests that in his love for the unglamorous Mrs Grey he is properly alive. If the motif of return retains a value here, it is in the idea of switching between two women: to return always involves one woman being cancelled out. And this in a novel by a woman who would spend many years writing her family history and yet, in all that time, she could never get beyond the period between her father's departure from their home when she was eight and his death when she was thirteen. Perhaps Rebecca West had the very best of reasons for wanting a return of the soldier, as the ones she knew weren't worth that much. This is what she had to say about them:

> 'Men are miserably poor stuff'
> 'Men are no damn use for anything'
> 'Men are all filth'
> 'All men are trash'

In other words, there is no doubting that she really loved a man. They disappointed only in not living up to the image of the man she was committed to.

If the 'return of the soldier' is a formula, it indicates perhaps the wish to resurrect a man: to make a new, changed man in the place of the old one. We find the motif in such stories as *The Return of Martin Guerre*, when someone returns, apparently, from the dead. A man is assumed lost, but he comes back, and even if the woman who had waited for him knows that he is not the same man as before, she allows him to step into the shoes of the latter. Although one may argue that this story articulates a male myth – one man steals the woman who is wed to another – the idea of returning into the place of an absent man is also close to the questions of female sexuality. The problem here is to reconcile this myth of one man taking the place of another with the commitment a woman may have to the one and only: although a woman's sexuality is never entirely directed to a man, the adoration of a single man is not infrequent. Whereas many men think of themselves as free even when they are married, a woman will often think of herself as tied to someone even if she is single or has merely a transitory lover.

Some women acknowledge quite directly that they have only had one great love, as they show some crumpled picture in an album or focus on an image in memory. Only one man counts, like Balzac for Mme de Berny, who would wait for him with her wheelchair moved to the window and die there with this last great wish unfulfilled once she knew that he would not come. Likewise, great male tragic heroes such as Heathcliff, men lost due to one special love in the past, bitter and disappointed due to their dashed hopes, are so often the creation of women. What matters is maintaining the belief that the man has a past, especially a past that involves another woman. Finding out that this is not the case may produce a devaluation of the man, as his dark secret dissolves into ordinary history.

This might appear to be a consequence of the Oedipus complex: whereas for the boy the romance ends when he accepts to give up the mother in exchange for access to other women, for the girl there is no such trade-off. She does not give up the mother for access to other men in the same way, and, as Geneviève Morel has pointed out, even if the father is valued, it would be a mistake to see the men in a woman's life as 'substitutes' for him, despite the fact that they may be chosen because they have certain traits in common with him (being older, being married etc.). The idea that a man is a replacement for another man is put in question even by the simple observation that a woman may genuinely love two men at the same time: it is not that one cancels the other out, as it often does in a man's relation to two women. To the bafflement of her male audience, George Sand could say that, of the two men in her life, she loved one 'more' and the other 'better'. And although the hatred a woman may feel towards a man is often explained in terms of the emergence of latent hostility towards the father, a man may be hated not because he's like the father but because he isn't. The echoing reproach is, 'Why aren't you different?' During the days of the suffragettes, Lord Weardale was attacked and assaulted at Euston Station by ladies under the impression that he was the Prime Minister, Mr Asquith. Speaking a few days later at a meeting, one of the most distinguished suffragettes said that 'it was very awkward for Lord Weardale that he should be so like Mr Asquith', and she continued to advise anyone who looked like a member of government to make some alteration to their appearance by growing a beard or moustache. 'Women,' she said, 'could not waste their time worrying over whether it was the right man or not.' Being the right man or not is indeed the crucial motif. And, in general, when hate arrives to blight the horizon of lovers, it is frequently linked to this accusation, 'Why aren't you someone else?' If there is a difference for men and women here, it may lie in the fact that the problem for the man takes the form of the invective 'Why aren't you someone else?', whereas for many women it becomes articulated in the thought 'You *are* someone else', for example, *not* the father or the mother.

Given this commitment to the one, why the recurring motif of the new, returned and changed man in the stories we have mentioned? To answer this question, we can start by exploring an apparently dissimilar image. In the myth of

Orpheus, a man journeys to the Underworld to rescue his dead wife, yet once she is on her way back to the world of the living, she is lost forever due to Orpheus' forbidden gesture of looking back. She has been lost once and now she is lost again. The story seems to be telling us something about a woman who is permanently lost. But why did Orpheus have to look back? In one version, after losing his wife this second time, he shuns the company of women and occupies himself exclusively with men, thus introducing homosexuality into Greece. His turning thus takes on a new sense: he looked, perhaps, in order not to see woman, a structure which we find also in voyeurism, which is concerned so often not with the reality of the naked body but with shadows and silhouettes. The look here does not aim at seeing something, but at not seeing something, or, more precisely, at seeing something which can't be seen, which is why it remains satisfied with shades and explains why men are so uninterested in women's clothes. The psychoanalytic idea here would be that what a man really doesn't want to know about is the truth of a woman's body, and this 'not wanting to know' is shifted, displaced to the woman's clothes, to give the illusion that he cares about her body, not what she's wearing.

Man's lack of attention here, his apparent failure to notice that his lover is wearing a new dress, is thus a kind of alibi against what he really does not want to have to confront. John Ruskin would spend many years in gentle appreciation of the objects of art and civilisation, and yet when the screen of the image was broken, he would run in terror from his marriage bed on seeing the naked body of his wife. As he politely put it, she 'was not formed to excite passion' as 'there were certain circumstances in her person which completely checked it'. Scholars debate whether this is a reference to menstruation or to the presence of pubic hair, but it shows Ruskin's horror at confronting the sex of his wife. After this, he could return his gaze to the register of the vanities, and the sculptures and paintings of women where the sex is glossed over. His retreat shows that renouncing women and being a fugitive from them are sometimes one and the same thing.

Although psychologists may subject such psychoanalytic arguments about the body to their scorn, it is difficult to deny that children have peculiar beliefs here, which are in no way banished from adult life. The belief in the woman's body having something which it doesn't have anatomically is, of course, the central Freudian supposition, and the story of Ruskin may serve as illustration, together with a wealth of clinical material collected by psychoanalysts. But psychology itself contains a mass of data on the very same issue: if one reviews the work of Piaget and his students, there is one problem that keeps coming back, the idea of object constancy. So many of Piaget's experiments are concerned with demonstrating how children analyse their environment into separate objects which still exist when they are hidden. The registration that an object endures when it can no longer be seen is understood as an important moment of child development, as if the crucial constitution of reality hinged on exactly this belief in a hidden element. Piagetian psychology is subject to much criticism today, yet the directions of its research are hardly accidental: child psychology and psychoanalysis share a strange but very real result, although one which they will no doubt continue to interpret in their separate ways. This faith in a 'fifth element', a hidden feature, may be seen clearly in the lives of those men who are drawn to the adventure of being urinated on by a woman. The urinary jet is made to emerge at the point the man perceives as a lack, a commitment that may take on many less spectacular forms. A man explains to his girlfriend that the penis is like a piece of wood, and that therefore she has to manipulate herself on top of him while he remains motionless. When she questions this strange idea, he tells her that it will allow her to 'come on him', an important condition for his own sexual enjoyment. When she then pointed out to him the ejaculatory conceit behind this quaint belief, he was non-plussed: what he wanted, she understood, was for her to come 'all over him', in exactly the form of a male ejaculation. With this realisation, her own interest faded, and she decided that the relationship would no longer do: rather than going out with a man, she said, she had just been going out with a man's problem.

Now, if Orpheus is a legend about a woman who does not come back, the return of the soldier narrative is, on the contrary, about someone who does come back, and indeed, many of the fictions written by women focus on this same motif of man's return. Cathy's amazement at the changed Heathcliff who returns to Wuthering Heights is a famous example of this radical transformation, as are the emergences of the long-lost brothers who pop up in the novels by Elizabeth Gaskell. The problem is in making sense of this return when the man is a new one, not simply the old lost love come back.

But perhaps this is less of a contradiction than it seems. If many women want to have a man who is changed, in that he loves them more, to have a changed man is to have a different one: hence he is doubled, as in the Martin Guerre story, and not simply modified a bit, as in West's *Return of the Soldier*. And yet, if doubled, he still has to be the same man, the place from which the woman can be loved. Would this be simply another version of the father? Is the man who comes back a fortified version of the father, one who loves his daughter without any obstacle? Here, things are less certain. It would be more accurate to say that the returning man isn't the father, but comes to occupy a place constructed out of the relation to him. As Lacan pointed out, what matters is the place from which a woman is loved, and a person or indeed something else, even a vampire or an alien, may be lodged there. When the soldier returns, it is from this underworld, and it is thus not surprising that once he's back, it is not long before he slips again into the shadows, as his place is not in the world of real live men but always somewhere in the distance.

Although this kind of return is so often imagined as the resurrection of a man, it may take on a rather different form, as the return not of a man but of something even bigger, like a house. In Daphne du Maurier's strange relation to the house she loved, Menabilly, she speaks time and time again of her desire to bring this place back to life. 'Menabilly would sleep on,' she wrote, 'like the sleeping beauty of the fairy tale, until someone should come to wake her.' Despite the fact that she knew that this house would never belong to her and that she could only rent it. It could never be fully possessed, and yet 'the house possessed me,' she said, 'as a mistress holds her lover'. Menabilly was her 'belle maison sans merci'. It has likewise often been pointed out that the main characters in her books are not people but places, from Jamaica Inn to the Manderley of *Rebecca*. When she first discovered Menabilly and began inquiring into its history, she was told that its last inhabitant had been married to a beautiful woman who had died, and into her place another and much younger woman had stepped. If this reminds one of the story of *Rebecca*, it still isn't enough to explain the strange relation to a house: if *Rebecca* was based, in some sense, on the Menabilly story, we need to pose the question of why this house should have mattered so much in the first place. The Menabilly fascination may be explained on one level in terms of the problem of feminine identity: when Daphne heard the story about the two women, it struck a chord with her own question of what it means to be a woman. In the *Rebecca* story, it means to go into the place of another woman. The ghost in the house, therefore, is that of the first wife.

But, as Daphne soon learnt, Menabilly had more to its history. In 1824 the skeleton of a man had been found in a walled-up section, with the shoes of a cavalier as its only signature. The identity of this unfortunate man had never been confirmed and Daphne would spend many hours searching the house to try to find the location of this lost section. The mystery would make her write an entire novel set in the Civil War period, with its own explanation as to the man's identity. She made of the skeleton the son of a great Royalist, giving up his life as a sort of act of sacrifice for his father. What this shows is that beyond the figure of the woman who was to haunt Menabilly, there was also that of the young man, the boy who gave up his life for his father. And indeed, it is this image that marked her first daydream of the house's owner: 'When I thought of him, it was not of an elderly man, a respectable justice of the peace, but of a small boy orphaned at two years old . . . watching his old grandfather with nervous doubting eyes.'

A house may thus be a monument for a woman, but there is someone else in there too. It is surely not an accident that the phrase Daphne used for her male persona in her correspondence describes exactly the secret of Menabilly: 'the boy in the box'. To follow the logic of our argument, the power of Menabilly may lie not just in Daphne's putting herself in the place of a woman who was once there, but in that of a boy who was once there. 'Menabilly was Manderley and Manderley was Menabilly,' she wrote. 'They were the same. Yet they had no likeness,' and we could add that this sameness and difference is reflected in the fact that one house has 'Men' in it and the other has 'Man'. Throughout her work, female characters continually voice the desire to be a son to a man: indeed, in every single novel that du Maurier published, there is at least one moment when a woman says she dreams of being a boy. And, in the narrative of her own life, she would say that she wished she could have been the son to her father. To her father's 'If only she'd been a boy', there is Daphne's echo 'If only I were a man.'

What this suggests is not the wish to be a boy, as some du Maurier commentators have argued, but something much more precise. Why would she want to be a boy, if this was not given a particular value by someone else: her father. There is thus a triangular relation, not just the dual images of Daphne and the boy. In fact, one could argue here that the wish to be a boy has nothing to do with masculinity and a lot to do with femininity: a woman who identifies with a man is often exquisitely feminine, due less to the traits she might borrow than to the actual act of imitation itself. It is the process of 'being like' which produces the feminine effect rather than the actual gestures or behaviour patterns imitated, as is seen in the fact that the more a man tries to 'be like' a man, the more feminine he becomes. In one of du Maurier's short stories, a woman puts on her lipstick in the presence of a group of men in a mountain hut in the middle of nowhere. She recognises the absurdity of the gesture yet she knows, all the same, that it will have an effect on the men. When St Cyprian explained his advice to women to wear makeup for the Resurrection, he said that otherwise God might not recognise them, but du Maurier's example shows that recognition itself is not the key factor. The respect for the register of the artificial, the 'being like', is what guarantees the effect, and it shows that it is not just a geographical context that makes lipstick matter.

There is thus no contradiction between du Maurier's feminine position and her continual reiteration of the wish to be a boy. Now, what does this relation tell us about the house, about Menabilly and Daphne's fascination with it? As the heroine of *Rebecca* writes, her father was her own 'secret property' just as Manderley was for her husband. What the house is to him, the father is to her, and yet we know that the house was of no small importance to Daphne herself. We might compare this with the famous return to a house in *Gone with the Wind*. Abandoned by Rhett Butler, Scarlett hears her father's words echoing in her head: 'Land is the only thing that matters, the only thing that lasts.' Rather than embroil herself in the loves of men, she chooses the home of her childhood, Tara, as the resting place for her desire. If a man's love was uncertain, the house was there as the point to return to after the whole cycle of her passions had spent itself. When Daphne first saw Menabilly, she felt the same certainty: the house, she says, 'made me hers upon the instant'.

But the question of a resting place was complicated by that of ownership, generating less a certainty than an insecurity. The fact that Menabilly could never be properly owned by her was thus a condition rather than an impediment to her interest: 'Perhaps it is the very insecurity of the love,' she would write, 'that makes the passion strong. Because she is not mine by right. The house is still entailed, and one day will belong to another.' Rather than belonging to her, it was Daphne who belonged to the house, another motif which runs like a red thread throughout her fiction. The characters have a lot of problems with other people, but they often feel a part of something that is bigger than them, be it the sea, a sunset or a family history. When it's a man, things are hardly so certain. A woman became particularly anxious when her ex-husband telephoned her to arrange the return of some clothes that remained in his flat. Although she wanted the garments, what mattered for her was the fact that a part of her remained close to him, that she belonged to him even in this one, last contingent way. Although she knew that she could never 'own' the man, her wish took the form of a belonging, and it is no accident that when a lover goes about the sad business of removing their things from the home of their ex-, they take the greatest care to forget at least one item, the sign that, at one level, a part of them is still close to the loved one.

The persistent vocabulary of lovers and mistresses used in connection with the house shows how deeply involved it is in a romance, and the impossibility of the house belonging to her might seem to suggest the unavailability of the father himself, prohibited for ever from his daughter. This implies, in turn, an answer to a peculiar problem in the du Maurier biography. Everyone close to the du Maurier family appeared to agree that little Daphne adored her actor-manager father and that their closeness was an unusually strong one. And yet it is surprising that when she was later given the chance to be even closer to him, to work with him in the theatre and on film, she made the decision to remain in Cornwall. What mattered to her was owning a boat and the mysterious Menabilly. But how could this strange torsion be accounted for? Wasn't everything for her organised around the father? Yet the choice of Cornwall does not necessarily contradict this. Perhaps she had found her own version of her father, her own way of elaborating the romance, now articulated outside her own flesh and blood family in the form of the house and the Slade family with whom she was deeply fascinated. Rather than renouncing the romance with the father, she simply took its conditions seriously: as the father would never fully belong to her, she found something else which would not fully belong to her, and it turned out to be a house. The title she selected as a child for her projected first novel describes this choice perfectly: *The Alternative*.

The first book she would actually publish is her own version of the Slade family history, which she called *The Loving Spirit*, and it features, besides the usual lovers, a boat, which would later metamorphose to become the Manderley of *Rebecca*. Janet Coombe marries her cousin Thomas, yet knows right from the start that she is divided between two things: the man, embodied by her husband, and something more important, difficult to define, which can take on the form of 'being a part of' the sea or what goes over it, a boat. When her son Joseph is born, she is certain that this is at last what she has been waiting for, and a love story between mother and son takes up the first part of the book. His dream is to build a ship with her name to it, and once the Coombe family has managed to do it, complete with figurehead depicting Janet, she dies at the moment it is launched. Her soul passes into the ship, just as in *Rebecca* the house becomes haunted by the shadow of the dead woman.

In both books, then, a woman has a special relation with a place and continues, after death, to possess it. What is so interesting here for our discussion of resurrection and return is that *The Loving Spirit* suggests that, obvious as it may sound, for something to be born, something has to die. This is a powerful unconscious motif in the lives of many women who become mothers: with pregnancy comes an inexplicable uneasiness with images of death, and the burgeoning of little superstitions. Even a woman who has only scorn for omens and signs may become superstitious in pregnancy. The reasons for this are linked to the relation of daughter to mother: and the daughter, in giving birth herself, may believe, at some level, that she will have to pay the price of her own death. As Helene Deutsch pointed out, the more pregnancy is experienced as a yearned for promise of future happiness, the more severely is the prospective mother threatened by the vengeance of fate. When the ship *Janet Coombe* is launched in *The Loving Spirit*, the real Janet Coombe disappears, and, many years later, it is her great-granddaughter Jennifer who conducts her own romance from inside the wreck of the ship. Uncannily close to the image of Janet on the figurehead, Jennifer comes into the place of this other woman in a special space, just as the heroine of *Rebecca* also goes into the place of another woman in the special space of Manderley. Both novels revolve around this relation of a woman to a place which houses something ghostly, and this gives us a clue as to why it is that if houses don't always come with ghosts, ghosts always come with houses.

It is indeed curious that ghosts nearly always like living in a house, and we speak more of haunted houses than of ghosts in their isolation. When a ghost is outside a house, it tends to become something else, like a vampire, a werewolf or some other demon. But a ghost needs a place, it is less free to roam around as much as its colleagues. In the great ghost stories, the central character is usually the house, not just the ghost itself, and in some versions, ghost and house are identified as one and the same. The house doesn't just contain the ghost, it is the demonic force itself. Rather than seeing this as a twist to revive a tired tradition, why not see it as revealing the dynamic that the tradition is built upon in the first place? But why should ghosts and houses go together hand in glove? The immediate response might be to say that it is simply a matter of displacement: the ill feelings we have about the inhabitant are transferred to the habitat. But one would then expect more of a separation of inhabitants from habitats. Otherwise, why should things just be done in halves? The ghost ought to disappear altogether. One might reply that the ghost remains because of a failure to displace all one's ill feelings to the habitat. It exists due to a failure to substitute entirely one thing for another. Which is certainly one of the most important characteristics of human sexuality: a failure of substitution, be it the failure to swop one object for another object or one desire for another desire. Thus the initial situation concerns shifting one's ill feelings, let's say, towards someone who is close to you, from them to their house. Since this doesn't succeed without some kind of remainder, what's left in the operation of displacement takes on the form of the ghost. Which makes sense. A ghost, after all, so often embodies a kind of free-floating ill will and it is always a question to determine, beyond their general malevolence, what exactly they want. In the story of haunted houses, it is thus the house that comes first, and then the ghost, and not the other way round.

As for birth and rebirth, these notions have certainly had a chequered history within psychoanalysis. The great exponent of a theory of the importance of birth was Freud's pupil Otto Rank, who has never had a good press. What is interesting in the case of Rank is the turning point, the moment that he became, to use a once popular analytic diagnosis, pseudo-imbecilic. Rank published a number of very readable and stimulating articles and books and then, suddenly, at a very precise date, his whole vision became contracted to one single and immensely stupid idea, the trauma of birth. In 1922 he is producing work of quality, such as the famous paper on 'Perversion and Neurosis'. He argues here that the idea that the aim of the sexual act is reproduction is entirely symptomatic. Confronted with the enigma of the sexual relations of the parents, Rank says, the idea of a child is inserted into this traumatic place as the solution to a mystery. Sex is given a meaning: the idea of having children. Sex and childbirth thus become inseparable, which might explain why neurotics don't like condoms. And since the child knows that it is impossible to have babies with the mother, the thesis becomes even more attractive due to its impossibility, now forcing the child along other psychic paths. Neurosis is defined as the clinging to this equation of sex with reproduction, and perversion and neurosis are contrasted in that the neurotic maintains his wish to *have* a child while the pervert strives to *be* one. Thus the accepted theory that the true aim of sex is reproduction is shown to be an infantile fantasy. Although one may find the seeds of Rank's later heresies within this article, it is still essential psychoanalytic reading, packed with interesting ideas and observations. And yet, only two years later, in his book *The Trauma of Birth*, he is claiming, in all seriousness, that the Bastille was stormed since it represented the mother's body, that bondage signifies the return to intrauterine immobility, that the mathematical attempts to square the circle were aimed at solving the problem of fitting into the womb, that the idea of a perpetual motion machine expressed the problem of dwelling in the womb, that Kant's thing-in-itself was the womb, that exhibitionism is a return to the nudity of the womb, that Socrates was the first person to overcome the trauma of birth by taking hemlock and, neither last nor least, the most scandalous of all of Rank's assertions, the claim that Goethe's dying words 'More light' were a reference to the glimpse of daylight on emerging from the womb at birth.

This phrase was always much debated by scholars: did it mean that Goethe was calling for the light of truth, or simply that he wanted someone to open the curtains? It is very difficult for us today to imagine the kind of hallowed state in which Goethe was held by the Viennese analysts, but it involved a reverence and respect which we rarely see bestowed on the literary and scientific figures of today. So great was this Goethe worship that when one of Freud's students was chatting with a friend in a Vienna street, on learning in the course of the conversation that some hardly significant letter of the Weimar poet was on display in the window of a nearby bookshop, he sped off instantly to read it, leaving his bewildered friend in mid-sentence. Imagine, then, the horror of the early analysts on reading Rank's note on 'More light', a reaction that would make of Rank's paragraph last words more definitive even than those of the beloved poet.

So what happened? Why did this awkward yet nonetheless talented lieutenant of Freud become so clueless? To start with, we need to see what position Rank held in Freud's circle. As Rank is lecturing one evening on the murder of kings, Freud passed a note to his cherished Lou Andreas-Salomé, which said, 'Rank disposes of the negative aspect of his filial love by means of this interest in the psychology of regicide: that is why he is so devoted.' And in her diary, Andreas-Salomé would write of this young man who would while away hours and days in a library researching his special interests, creation, birth and the mentor relation that he is 'a son and nothing but a son'.

This filial position, powerful as it may seem, fails to find an obvious reflection in the book about the trauma of birth, where the central place is given to mother and child, and the mentors are exclusively feminine. As Freud pointed out to him, there is no place for the father in this work. The key to understanding this strange twist is in the chronology. There's Rank, working out all his filial problems, entrenched in his position as a son, when suddenly, in April 1923, he hears, together with all the rest of the analytic community, that Freud has cancer, and is not expected to live much longer. What happens now was decisive not just for Rank but for many of Freud's students: with the idea of the master's death made concrete, the question of succession became very real. In other words, the symbolic relations of father to son had to be confronted in raw form. And to this, Rank replied not with another lecture on regicide but a theory that reduced everything, and really everything, to the relation of mother and child. Where the symbolic relation of father–son failed to be articulated, the imaginary idea of mother–child came into its place. Although Freud was not to die for another sixteen years, Rank's failure of will here is evident in the choice of his own time of death: only one month after that of his master.

It might be objected that Rank has really had an unfair press, and that the theory of the trauma of birth is not simply a sad contraction of human knowledge. Isn't it true, after all, as women often point out, that a man is a sort of 'baby-hero', oscillating between these two quite disparate positions? Where Rank's earlier work had been entitled *The Myth of the Birth of the Hero*, the trauma of birth book could have been called quite appropriately *The Myth of the Birth of the Baby*. Can anything, then, be rescued from these pages? A man detailed his fascination with the cycle of *Die Hard* films in pinpointing the many scenes in which Bruce Willis is seen crawling around in narrow pipes. He always seems to be caught in this hollow machinery of large structures like skyscrapers and airports. If one happened to be of Rankian persuasion, it would be yet another example of the return to the womb thesis: the buildings equal the mother and the narrow spaces equal the womb or the path to and from it. How else could one account for this recurring feature of these popular films?

To answer this question involves not simply an impeachment of the birth trauma theory, but also adds to the problem of rescue we have been discussing. Whereas so many films in the late seventies and early eighties were concerned with 'disasters', in which a group of stars found themselves in the wrong place, from the mid-eighties on there was a burgeoning of films in which one person succeeded in rescuing a group of trapped people from terrorists. In the earlier disaster movies, the rescuing team had a much less important role to play in the narrative and they tended to battle not with a band of terrorists with state of the art weapons but rather with the prejudices and greed of some business concern. In the rescue film, it is one person who has to get everyone else out of trouble, and whereas in the disaster movie the emphasis was generally on the *guests* being in the wrong place at the wrong time, it is now a question of the *rescuer* being in the wrong place at the wrong time. This is the key to the *Die Hard* cycle: it is not just the resilience of the hero that matters, but the fact that he is always in the position of someone who shouldn't be there, who is there by accident, a spanner in the works for both police and thugs. And the villains in these films are impeccably educated: they have good manners, dress well and quote classical authors. The rescuing hero, on the contrary, is brutish, thus setting up a tension between the two forces. When Abraham wrote his paper on rescue fantasies, he made one important observation which he did not really explain. He noticed that at the beginning of *Oedipus Rex* by Sophocles, Oedipus meets the carriage of Laius by chance. Although the subsequent events are well known – the killing of the father and incest with the mother – this note of contingency has a special value. In the rescue films, it takes the form of the chance 'being there' of the hero, which is opposed to the fine web of planning that the terrorists have spent so long perfecting. If the terrorists have tried to think of everything, all possible contingencies, bluffs and double bluffs, the one thing their linguistic system has not bargained on is the ineffable presence of the clumsy policeman. There is thus a tension between a system, carefully constructed by the educated terrorists, and the spanner in the works, the non-linguistic element that takes the form of the brute presence of the hero. All the shinnying about in pipes and air-vents thus takes on a sense not in terms of child manoeuvring inside mother's body, but of non-linguistic object making ripples in a linguistic system, eventually causing it to collapse. The towerblocks and airports, after all, are embodiments of technologies, masses of information and circuitry that incarnate knowledge. The hero becomes a hero due to his disruption of this knowledge, in the form both of the edifice itself and of the terrorists' plan.

In *Die Hard*, Bruce Willis fits in neither with the plans of the villains nor of the police: he is the perfect illustration of something that shouldn't be there, and this suggests a further response to the question of rescue. If becoming a rescuer depends in these films on such a position, it implies that it is not in a plan or a knowledge that one will find a place in fantasy. The hero takes on his value at exactly the point that the plans of the terrorists and the police *do not recognise him*, where they fail to give him a place. It is from this point of not having a place in a network of knowledge that the rescuer takes on his position. If we wished to give to the rescue stories of such films the status of phantasies proper as they are met with in psychoanalysis, it is in this sense of an identity taking on its consistency at the point that language fails to recognise one. It is at the point where one does not fit in, where one is not recognised by a discourse, that something from another register is introduced: in this case, the policeman whose manners contrast so much with that of the polished and educated villain. His function is not to speak, but to be the object shuttling around in the recesses of a building, and it is this position which, in the *Die Hard* cycle, gives the rescuer his real identity. Although for everyone else he shouldn't be there, because he always is, he takes on an identity as 'The person who shouldn't be there but always is': his being, his identity, is thus defined in terms of what doesn't fit in with something else. If this can tell us something about the rescue fantasy, it is that the position of the protagonist is rooted at the point where, in some discourse, he is not recognised. This has a profound effect on even the sweetest people. When someone is snubbed or insulted in some way, it often releases the most appalling daydreams of revenge: the mild-mannered employee is kept awake at night with images of how he or she ought to have acted in the encounter with their boss or colleague. The search for what they ought to have said, the witty remark or counterexample, quickly becomes transformed into scenes of torture and destruction. A pleasant and harmless office worker explained his lack of sleep in exactly these terms: after a colleague had completely failed to register his contribution to an important project, he had at first run through in his mind the countless possible replies he could have made but didn't. After that came a series of gruesome scenes in which the colleague was being torn apart by wild horses and then flayed. What this shows is how fantasy is built up at precisely those points where we are not recognised, where we have no place, as a response, a way to guarantee our own subjectivity. If we then remember that as children most of life must have consisted in not being recognised in some way (on the immediate level – it is a sibling or the other parent who is recognised instead), we can assume the existence of a whole set of nasty thoughts, of which, in our conscious life, we are blissfully unaware.

There is one more aspect of the idea of rescue for a woman that we have not yet discussed. In *The Loving Spirit* we saw how important it was for the heroine to feel 'a part' of something else, some force or spirit that was different from a real man. To rescue and to be rescued separate here, and it may be the case that when a woman has the desire to be rescued it is in this sense of becoming a part of something beyond her. A girl would spend many evenings staring at the golden stars painted on the ceiling of her room, certain that there was something there, what she would later on call 'a third force'. Throughout the involved histories of her relations with men, her disappointments were always set against the knowledge that there was something else, waiting and watching, something that had absolute confidence in her. George Sand told a similar story. Precocious as a child and quick to learn, the one problem that perplexed her family was her inability to succeed with the common alphabet: she could say everything except the letter 'b' (pronounced 'bé' in French). Neither punishment nor prayer could induce her to correct the elision. When she was twelve, a strange thing happened: in a dream the letters of the alphabet settled in the form of the word 'Corambé'. She knew at once that this word was to accompany her, observing her behaviour, consoling her, a presence which would sustain her and to which she would relate long stories. If she could run through a series of male lovers in her later life, this private deity would remain constant in her youth. To Corambé she would build an altar, pray and commune. In her discussion of Sand's life, Helene Deutsch links the 'coram' of 'Corambé' with the Latin *coram*, 'in the presence of', and one might add that *coram* is found most famously in the liturgical *coram deo*, 'in the presence of God'. Now, if 'bé' is the 'b' of her childhood alphabet, 'Corambé' means 'in the presence of b', where the letter 'b' takes the place of the God. The scandals of her abundant love life are thus shadowed by this silent partner, just as for the heroine of *The Loving Spirit*, there is a split between the real men in her life and the force to which she feels she belongs, the site of her true fidelity. This duality is often misunderstood, as the relation to men is used to interpret the relation to what is beyond them. Thus commentators on the great female mystics of the middle ages are often struck by how their encounters with God seem like a big orgasm. But such descriptions are in fact quite rare. As the historian Carol Walker Bynum pointed out, most female mystic writing is less about the ecstasy of union than about the *impossibility of ever being fully alone*. This impossibility can take the name of 'Corambé' or the 'loving spirit' or the 'third force', but it is always different from a man.

If love between humans doesn't always last, these strange objects do endure. The 'loving spirit', 'Corambé' and the 'third force' are names of something that is there whatever happens in the vicissitudes of a history, and thus take on the function of a sort of guarantee, something that can be trusted. It is perhaps into the space established by these private deities that a promise can take on its sense. But this is not likely to be a promise coming from a real man. Rather, one could say that the place of this third term is itself the result of a broken promise in the past. George Sand's 'Corambé' would appear only after a series of terrible disappointments from her mother, as the secret project of leaving her grandmother for a life alone with the mother came to grief. For the guarantee to emerge, for the 'third force' to always be there, constant and faithful, something was perhaps once not so certain. If the 'loving spirit' can never disappoint, perhaps it comes into the place of something that did disappoint, something that either didn't last or never happened at all. Where words failed, something else was elected into their place. One love story thus supposes another, and for a romance to begin, there is always the question of how, exactly, the last one ended.

Four

Reik once said that there is no such thing as a love story, because love is always a story within a story. Each history carries with it a more ancient one, recreated, retranscribed, reorganised perhaps, affecting our pasts, our presents and our futures. Bertrand Russell recalled his amazement one day on finding an old diary of his father which recorded the details of his courting and engagement, identical in almost every detail with Russell's own relations with his first wife. Although he had not been consciously aware of any repeat performance, he had nonetheless played it out with more fidelity than he ever showed to his partners. If a love story has its roots in the past, there is the question of how this will affect its future, and, crucially, how its beginning will reflect its end.

A history, as each psychoanalysis shows, does not just repeat itself, it rhymes. A woman remembers the first moment she caught sight of the man she would love, standing motionless on a street in Rome, gazing at her and then gradually moving towards her. Years later, the scene that marks their farewell rejoins this past. Their eyes meet in the same street, he moves towards her, but this time she turns and walks away. The scene stays the same, but now she subtracts herself from his gaze, and knows that their romance is over. St Augustine could write that 'if you wish to know what is the nature of love, look to where it leads', but the example shows that it is equally important to look to where it starts. A man who chooses a Tarkovski film for a first date might understand, at some level, that the issue of the relationship to which he aspires won't be a bright one, and this choice of contexts might tell you more about the future than any promise.

A date, after all, is an organisation. Someone is inserted into a framework which is never without a meaning, and this context will give a clue to the set of their interests. Urging a trip to the cinema, for example, might mean that what matters is the image, whereas a visit to a restaurant might suggest a priority given to the act of devouring. A night out dancing might mean that what matters is being seen by others or to see others beyond the partner. When a London newspaper decided on its date of the year, the elegant and special lady received a number of propositions, and chose the one that most intrigued her. Yet when push came to shove, the man seemed more interested in showing her to his friends than in exploring her being, giving them the priority over a candlelit dinner. Even with the success of securing the rendezvous, what mattered was demonstrating it not simply to himself but to others, and the lady was understandably keen to end his fiesta early.

One night stands do not always follow first dates, but when they do a similar imbalance repeats itself. A one night stand is both the first and the last time that something happens, even if this fact is not known by all parties concerned. In fact, it often only becomes a one night stand many nights later, when the full signification that it won't happen again has been set into place. What seems a beginning to the one lover is a full stop to the other. The problem here is that human beings are not very good at full stops: they prefer perhapses to endings, commas and clauses to curtains. And if there is indeed a certain symmetry between beginnings and endings, would this mean that relations which begin surgically (love at first sight) will end surgically? This is not so sure, but the frameworks chosen for beginnings will nevertheless become sharper, more separate at endings. When Chairman Mao was asked, late in his life, to evaluate the effects of the French Revolution, he replied that it was too early to say, but in the field of love a history may begin with the clues to its own solution. Whatever the activity chosen for the first encounter, a reason is present which excludes the partner at some unconscious level. When the relationship ends, the same principle of exclusion will often become clear, and the initial elements which were prioritised over the partner come into focus properly. Although such endings may not be as absolute as that of the sovereign herself, the motto of Mary Stuart condenses this symmetry: 'In my end is my beginning.'

A young woman shows up at the opening of an art exhibition and a stranger approaches her in the crowded room. His first words to her are 'Welcome to my show.' Within a few months they are living together, and she remains by his side to accompany him through his changing moods and the moving sands of his profession. Two years later, she wakes up one morning and hears the same words that marked the beginning of their partnership echoing in her head: 'Welcome to my show.' The words made precise her uneasiness over several months, her role as the woman he shows to the world, hindered in her own life, her opportunities blocked, existing precisely as just a part of his show, and it is these words that once served as introduction that now signal exit. The detail that marks the beginning contains the structure of an end.

One might argue that in this case the decision had been made, and the woman searched back in her past to find something that could simply make her misgiving concrete, a marker for her misery and a sign for her discontent. In a tender moment beneath the stars shortly after their marriage, Katharine Hepburn's mother asked her husband if he was interested in hearing her innermost thoughts. When he said no, she began to direct her loathing to his necktie, and would make it the focus of her disparaging remarks for several hours. The detail here seems contingent, a sign of something else. It could have been anything – his necktie, his shoes, his fingernails – and not, as in the earlier example, the very words that were there at the start. But the actual detail *does* matter. Whether this necktie had a future in their relationship is unclear, although one might conjecture that since it was there at the start, it would reappear later on. The link between endings and beginnings is indeed powerful. If something begins well, that doesn't mean that it will end well, and if it begins badly that doesn't mean that it will end badly, but it does mean that the *details* which were there at the start will be there at the end. The villain in the cartoon series *Scooby Doo* is always the first insignificant character that we meet, until his identity is revealed in the famous unmasking scene at the end. Although everyone knows that this is how things will work out, the narrative never changes, so compelling is the logic that links start to finish. Like the mazes of antiquity, the point of entry is the same as the point of exit. And in love, the things which were most cherished in the partner will ultimately be the things that are the most despised. To cherish, to love and to hate, we start with the little things. The Puritans first attacked the square hats and rockets of the bishops, and then the bishops themselves. And when we find hate here, it is in exactly those places where we would expect to find love: in a family, for example, or between lovers, but always linked to the details through which love first articulated itself, the words at the art opening or the gaze on the street in Rome. Which means that any theory of passion should also include a theory of details.

Why should what is so small matter in something which is so big? It is surely no accident that the biggest film ever ıe, Kevin Costner's *Waterworld*, starts with one of the nallest things ever made, a shot of the actor peeing. From this modest beginning springs the whole aquatic universe, and it is amusing to note how the most sophisticated feats of modern film-making forever remain grounded in the boy's concern with liquids. What boys have to accept, however, is that their capacity to generate liquid is always limited. In their passage through the Oedipus complex, it is a question of registering the fact that virility is a promise for the future: the service of the mother is given up in return for the idea of receiving something at a later date from the father. It's a trade off: something is renounced for an expectation, a desire, which is no doubt the reason why pubescent boys from time to time shave off their pubic hair with such enthusiasm. If the pubes are sacrificed now, more will grow in their place in the future. Virility, as Lacan said, is thus based on castration, and we can remember here how superheroes only become superheroes after some accident, being bitten by a spider or damaged in a fall or a crash. The scientists who turned Lee Majors into the Six Million Dollar Man could only do this *after* he had been injured, after he had lost something.

The problem with all this is that when boys do have something, since having is linked with this kind of anticipation, it is often not easy for them to assume it in the present. They get worried about not having it or its not being there. Perhaps that's why men wear the same clothes for weeks on end and don't like taking their shoes off: with something to lose, they don't want to take any chances. But some men are more worried than others, and not everyone has the same relation to oedipal ambition. There must be a difference between the boy who spends his time nagging for a real battleship and the boy who just wants to make a model of it. A congress of scale model makers has a strange tranquillity about it, as if there was an acceptance of the oedipal relation, 'I'll settle for a smaller model', a copy which is reduced in relation to the original. The details have to be the same, but the scale registers a symbolic limit. When Tom Hanks grows overnight in *Big*, his physical size is still not enough to equip him for taking on the role of a man. After spending the night with a woman for the first time he can drink black coffee, but the more he gets involved, the more he yearns to return to his former size and be with his mummy. He has learnt, by the end of this fiction, that accepting one's size is better. It is thus less a question of striving to have the bigger fish, than of mapping it, symbolically, to smaller scale, and being content with something imperfect. Freud's son Martin recalled fondly that on the only occasion on which his father had gone to buy groceries, he returned with an enormous salami in his knapsack, adding with reverence that 'the salami evidently created a strong impression on us children'. How different from the passions of those men who want nothing but the bigger fish for themselves. Hemingway's offer to compare the size of his organ with that of the worried F. Scott Fitzgerald in the men's room of a Paris café was a contest which could have taken politer forms: when the Earl of Northumberland learnt that Buckingham drove six horses in his coach, he immediately passed through the city with eight. Fitzgerald, to follow his example, could have written longer books. If the model maker contents himself with the scaled-down copy, he quietly sidesteps the dangers of scaling-up. When Clarendon and Wolsey built their enormous houses, it was seen as a state crime: these ministers, unable to remove themselves from the battle of forms, paid the price for their unhealthy ambitions.

This relation of the big and the small, the love story and the detail, has often been tackled by psychologists. At the start of our lives, we relate to someone who represents, in part, a set of qualities (the timbre of voice, the smell of skin, the colour of hair). In other words, a process of abstraction operates, which fixes in the psyche a collection of qualities or traits. When our emotions are displaced and transferred later on, they are transferred through exactly these qualities. It is the detail, the single abstracted trait that will direct the transfer of libido. A woman who has had a number of relationships notes the way in which each new lover only becomes attractive if they have what she calls 'a kindly face', a detail, a description which thus organises her emotional life. Love doesn't just glorify certain details of the partner, it depends entirely on their presence, as the crystals will depend on the bough. But why should these details work sometimes and not all of the time? Why doesn't the presence of a certain colour hair or a certain perfume automatically make us fall in love? If all that mattered was the evocation of a certain discrete set of traits, love would be a mechanistic operation, switched on and off at precise times, and calculable in advance. Which, as everyone knows, is false. Fetishism is not love for the reason that it relies on just one precise trait that is necessary for sexual enjoyment. If loving involves more, why does it happen only sometimes? And why sometimes only once?

It is perhaps an irony that love can be defined as both paying attention to details and ignoring them. Some aspect of the loved one – a kindly expression, a lock of hair – will take on an exaggerated importance at the start of love, but several other aspects will, at a conscious level, be ignored. In Fritz Lang's film *Secret Beyond the Door*, it is through a tiny detail that the relation of the lovers is filtered. Celia, a wealthy society girl, has little interest in the men that the New York calendar has to offer her, and on a trip to Mexico she meets the disturbed architect Mark Lamphere.

They marry, yet the honeymoon is interrupted when he vanishes with a feeble excuse, arranging to meet her later at his home near New York, Lavender Falls. The whole place is a bit sinister and there is no Mark there when she arrives. As he is due in on the train, she decides to go to meet him, and at the station she picks some flowers. The moment he catches sight of them he goes into a trance and leaves. This is all too much for the new bride, and she soon makes up her mind to leave him. But, when she thinks about her situation, she reconsiders. She's got no one else to turn to, and she still wants, she says, to be everything for him. They decide that a big housewarming party is just the thing required to create a bit of warmth, and it is now that she begins to discover one of Mark's darker secrets.

He has constructed a collection of rooms in one of the wings of Lavender Falls, each one a replica of the scene of a famous murder. Each room, he explains to his guests, tells a story and he muses that it is the room rather than the people inside it which determines the actions of its characters. It is obvious that Mark has a twisted kind of satisfaction in talking about the gruesome crimes, and his tour continues until they reach room number 7. Which is out of bounds. Naturally, she's got to know what's in this room, and when she eventually manages to sneak inside, she is horrified to see that it is a replica of her own bedroom. This is all too much, and she quite wisely runs out of the house. A scream is heard, and then, in the film's excellent twist, we find that she has gone back. Not only has she gone back into the house, she has gone into the very room that is prohibited, the room that is presumably the site of her own murder.

In a sense, she has realised that if she wants to have any effect on her unusual husband, it will not be from the outside, in talking rationally with him or trying to influence him, but only from within the very phantasy frame he has constructed. Waiting for him in the room, she has put herself into the very place in which his murderous desire has situated her. And realising that Mark had gone into his trance at the station the moment he saw the flowers, she picks the same ones again, clasping them as he approaches her. He moves towards her like an automaton, when suddenly everything becomes clear. In the background there had been the sound of a door locking, and she realises that the same sound had triggered his bizarre behaviour on their honeymoon. As she links the material, he remembers visiting his mother's room as a child, and the sound of the door being locked. His own door had also been locked as the mother went out dancing with a man, although he now discovers, thanks to Celia, that it had been his sister and not his mother who had locked him in. The lilacs that affect him so strongly are indexes of the mother, cut out at Lavender Falls after her death, and thus each time he sees them he is taken back to the scene in which he is separated from the enjoyment of the mother and her dancing partner. The fascination with murder scenes and his own homicidal propensities towards Celia perpetuate his desire to avenge this exclusion.

What the film shows so eloquently is how the key relations in someone's life are organised through details – the flowers, the noise of the door locking – of which there is no conscious awareness. They operate at an unconscious level, to produce feelings that are indeed conscious but which are not linked properly to their cause. When Mark feels murderous or angry or the need to vanish, he may think he knows why, but the real reasons, linked to the operation of the details, are unknown to him. And what Celia has understood is that to effect all this, she has to put herself *inside* its framework. In her gesture of returning to the forbidden room, she has put herself in the place of the flowers, as the object that will cause his desire. Just as the flowers had affected him so powerfully, she desires herself to have the same effect: rather than avoiding the framework set up by the details, she therefore puts herself inside it. Rather than wishing to be loved for herself, for what she is, she realises that she has to be loved first for what she isn't, she has to alienate herself to the framework of his phantasy and it is only then that there will be any possibility for a real adjustment in their relationship. If what she wants is a changed man, she has to change herself into the space built up by his phantasy, and then make the right causal connections with his past. In other words, she has to do an inside job.

The big question, of course, is, What will happen now that the man has had the relation to his phantasy clarified? In a sense, Celia's work is merely preparatory: there is the further question of how someone can then be taken outside their phantasy and what effects this will have. The Hollywood version is more than a touch ideal, but the future of Mark and Celia will now presumably have a new set of problems. If her detective work releases him from his homicidal passion, how will he love her now, given that the murderous framework of his phantasy is what gave her such a value for him in the first place? We can remember that even before the story of the rooms, when he first sets eyes on her in Mexico, it is in exactly this context: she has just been missed by a knife thrown in a lovers' quarrel. The lethal condition is there all along. Would it then be correct to say that when such a framework for a man is put in question, his partner loses her brilliance and becomes often little more than an object of indifference or hate? But different things can happen here. If passionate love ends, other forms of companionship can begin, without any magical disappearance of a phantasy.

In *Indecent Proposal*, a film written and produced by women, we see both this endurance of a bond between lovers and the giving up of another love story. Demi Moore and her husband take a trip to Las Vegas in the hope of cheating their economic difficulties and completing the dream house that the young architect has designed. Since he is not as bizarre as Mark Lamphere, there's no replica of a murder room in it, and they just want to enjoy happy times there. As Demi is admiring a dress, she purloins a handful of chocolates, unaware that she is being watched by a man who is rich enough to buy a whole chocolate factory. When he offers to buy her the dress, rather than politely refusing and going on her way, her curiosity is aroused and she asks him why he'd want to do that. Robert Redford replies that she has earned it as he enjoyed watching her, to give a not uncommon instance of exchange: Demi's own lack, made present by her interest in the dress and the chocolates, is given a monetary value. Her lack equals his enjoyment, and the basic circuit of exchange is set up.

As she imagined herself in that dress, she incarnated the aspect of a woman who desires something out of reach, something beyond herself. Unable to take on the dress as her own, she took the chocolates instead, but what the man wants here is to become the beyond for her himself, to provide her with it. If Robert Redford had been so inclined, he could have bought the dress and worn it himself, and the film could have kept the same title. Instead, he wants to complete her in a different way, to *give* her the things she doesn't have, a function which is complicated when we remember that Demi in fact has a husband, a man she loves. After this initial encounter, husband and wife play the gaming tables and succeed in losing everything they have won. And now the rich man intervenes again: he proposes a swap involving his desire, one night with Demi in exchange for one million dollars.

If that seems reasonable, we ought to remember that just

before the proposition Demi had thrown the dice for the rich man at the gaming tables, and he had thus become himself one million dollars richer. In a sense, he is only giving what he had thanks to her: she bet with a sum that didn't belong to her, and now he offers it back, yet via a strange route. Accepting the trade, she spends the night with Robert Redford, but it is only when the exchange is formally complete that Demi begins to realise that things have only just started. Since swapping is not a simple business: it is not just one night for one million, since a night can become eternal, its effects haunting the couple's life well beyond daybreak. Redford can tell them that 'the night would come and go but the money would last a lifetime', yet it is exactly the opposite that occurs. As the relation of husband and wife thus starts to dissolve, the rich man continues his pursuit, and Demi only begins to soften once he makes it clear that he needs her. In other words, that this man who has everything lacks something, and she becomes equivalent to what it is that he lacks. And soon, she leaves house and home for the rich man's more splendid one.

There is thus both a beginning and an ending, or so it would seem. For Redford, something begins when he looks at Demi: she is caught up in the framework of his phantasy which no doubt privileges the field of vision. She becomes the object he wants to complete, saturating what is unsatisfied in her with what he can purchase. And for her and her husband, something ends, as the shadow of exactly this lack of satisfaction comes to darken their lives. The husband not only confronts the fact that there is something beyond him, but this something takes on the consistency of another man, one who's got more than he does. Curiously enough, it is after this distancing that another object starts to take on a special value, not a woman but a brick. Returning to a passion of the past, the husband now lectures on architecture, and we witness a powerful encomium on the virtues of this common piece of stone, the trivial base on which the miracles of architecture have been constructed. Like Stendhal's bough, it is on this that crystals are formed, and from one contingent element we move to another, this time not a brick but something larger though equally ineffable: a hippopotamus. Demi and her new companion are at a charity auction to raise money for wildlife in danger. The rich bid for the salvation of selected beasts, and when the hippo is put up for auction, Redford proposes a modest sum, until a voice outdoes his offer with the bid of one million dollars. It is, of course, the husband, wagering the very sum that he had received in such an unusual way from Redford. Husband and wife talk, and as she drives away from the auction with Redford, the rich man understands that something is over. His riches are for once matched by his ingenuity, and he contrives on the spur of the moment a means to let her escape, trivialising her worth by evoking the rest of the fictitious series of women he has had for the same wager. She takes the cue, gets out of the car and refinds her husband in an especially tender scene. And now Redford explains the moment of his choice.

As Demi and her husband talked at the auction, he knew that 'she would never have looked at me the way she looked at him'. In other words, that it was ultimately impossible for him to go into the shoes of another man, that he could buy everything with a price, but limits don't have prices, and thus the slave, not the rich man, has something the other can never have. The beauty of the sequence lies in the passage from brick to hippopotamus, two brute, senseless objects which function as the stake for what happens in the field of love. The husband pays one million for a hippopotamus, just as Redford paid one million for a woman. In this rude symmetry, perhaps what Redford understood was that what counted for him was less the woman than the other man, and that the woman, with all her charms, was simply an object in the operation that really mattered to him, the act of exchange itself. Exchange is no simple matter, since it always produces a surplus, a remainder, which after the initial act was what tormented the life of the couple, the fact that the night with the rich man was something that didn't go away. The real indecent proposal, in this sense, is less the proposition of the rich man than the bid of one million for the hippopotamus, indecent in that it reveals the real mechanics of desire and exchange.

Where anthropologists have argued that the principal object of exchange in our history has been woman, traded as the link between two social groups, the privileged example today is not woman but footballer. Shifted from one tribe to another at astonishing cost, these mobile players demonstrate the autonomy of the economic circuit, but, with the crucial difference from familial exchange, they do not serve to cement relations between two groups. If a player moves from Manchester to Newcastle, the teams are not bound in an alliance, and it is no doubt the effort of the player to convert this solitude into kinship with his new mates. If bonds do issue, they are in the reflected form of the exchange of football cards, the images of the players which change hands between children. It is always an important moment when children enter this circuit, when their concerns move from exclusive possession of a toy to a game as such, which involves exchange and trading. Children like swapping things, but what this shows is that the basic swap has already taken place: giving up the mother for a place in the symbolic network. Playing at 'Monopoly' means that the original monopoly of the mother has been broken, and the symbolic circuit reached in which one item can be exchanged for something else. When dragons are killed in fairy tales, the glory of the murderous action obscures the real stake of the narrative: besides chewing up knights, dragons guard treasures, and, as has often been pointed out, to kill a dragon is to set the treasure back into economic circulation. As the gold changes hands, so does the other prize in dragon-slaying, the princess who can now leave her family to marry the slayer. For anything to enter the exchange circuit, some dragon has to be killed, an action which, as the Oedipus complex shows, is neither simple nor happy. Today, we might not believe in dragons, but we continue to speak about them in referring to the mother-in-law. Whereas the legends of medieval times give a privileged place to these adventures of dragon-slaying and malign family relations, they are rarer today, and have passed into the technology of video games. Huizinga once wrote a book called *The Waning of the Middle Ages*, but with the demise of dragons and evil in-laws in our literature, it might be updated as *The Waning of the Mother-in-Law*.

Or, *From Dragons to Details*. This is one of the things that phantasy does, moving the otherness of another human being's sexuality into a carefully constructed framework, one which is established, as we have seen, partly through the function of details. But if this is one way to explain love, there is still the question of why we fall in love at the times we do. Popular wisdom has it that when someone is deeply disappointed, they can do two things: go shopping or entertain some enthusiasm for a cause, like loving someone or something else, a person or an abstract idea. But things are slightly more complicated. What Freud and his students found was that there has to be something like a *readiness* to fall in love, an initial state more discreet than its successor yet essential in its presence. Falling in love will not be a complete accident, even if meeting the person you cherish involves a certain degree of chance.

Freud focused on the form of love called transference, and he tried to formulate some of its conditions. In popular expositions, transference is supposed to be when we shift our feelings towards a parent or some important figure from the past to someone else in one's present. Although it might be argued that this is not really the same as true love, the more it is investigated, the more it takes on exactly this dignity: both, after all, are based on illusion, but that doesn't make them any the less real. If there is a difference here, it is that if someone in love meets their loved one by chance in a café, they may well be delighted and happy (provided the loved one is not with someone else), but if they meet their analyst any delight will probably be mixed with fear or even a bit of anxiety. If we take transference as a starting point to explore this readiness to love, we have to ask why it occurs when it does and what, exactly, gets it going.

The basic problem is simple enough: unconscious complexes are not too happy to be revealed, and yet analysis aims at accessing them in some way. Often, their only traces may be in some apparently insignificant derivative: a man with an appetite for fruit pastilles could eat all of them apart from the yellow ones, an exclusion which indexed a chain of associations blocked out from consciousness. As the derivatives of the complex are elaborated – the more he spoke about what the word 'yellow' made him think of – the tension increases, and a very peculiar thing happens. In order to safeguard itself, the unconscious complex will release some of its parts, the parts which most satisfy the initial resistance to becoming conscious. Thus, rather than continuing to link associations from the yellow fruit pastille to some unpleasant idea, the patient will experience a new sentiment towards the analyst. He may suddenly entertain tender or hostile thoughts, at the very place where the chain of associations ought to be continuing. In other words, a part of the unconscious complex affiliates itself to the idea of the analyst. As an example of this process, it is often the case that when a woman can establish amorous transferences onto men quickly, one can bet that there is a real problem with the mother, whereas if the transferences are made quickly to women, there will be a major problem with the father. Although this simplifies things too much, what the generalisation shows is how transferences do not 'tell the truth', and how the ease with which they seem to emerge is the sign that a resistance is being satisfied rather than an unconscious complex really being accessed: a feeling, however genuine it may seem, is coming into the place of something else.

The analyst may now find himself the apparent object of feelings that seem to come from nowhere, as big emotions come to convulse the quiet ritual of sessions. The big mistake, and the mistake made by generation after generation of analysts, is to interpret the transference as such systematically, to assume that if the patient's associations seem to refer to their own person, this should be pointed out, and that this, in effect, is what analysis is all about. If the patient feels sad on a Monday, it may be interpreted, on this model, as being due to the separation from the analyst over the weekend. Or if they are happy, it's because they're glad to see them. This is really quite similar to how parents treat a baby. Whatever the infant does, it is interpreted as being somehow linked to them: 'It's trying to say (to me) . . .', 'It's smiling (at me)', etc. In other words, everything is understood as a response to something that *they* do. Yet although Freud insisted that battles could not be fought *in absentia*, he showed how the ideas linked to the analyst are being brought into the foreground in order to keep the rest of the complex out of the picture. Thus rather than always interpreting the material as being a sort of commentary on the patient's feelings towards the analyst, however obvious this may seem, it would be more prudent to approach it as referring to something beyond the analyst, thus allowing the possibility of an analysis of the latter part of the complex, the elements that are enigmatic and off field. This is the idea, elaborated by Lacan, of trying to aim at something beyond the 'meaning' of the patient's speech, a point where speech is lacking which can be evoked rather than referred to directly.

A patient spoke in her session of her efforts throughout the day to recall the name of a particular household product. She described it in such a way that it was clear what the product was, and the name of this product, as it happened, was a perfect anagram of the name of her analyst. The classical response might well have consisted here in interpreting, introducing the forgotten name and pointing out its identity with the analyst's proper name, with the suggestion that what the patient was really thinking about all along was her analyst. The Freudian idea, however, implies something slightly different, and in this instance, rather than interpreting, I encouraged further associations. When the name was recalled, in between sessions, it led on to a series of associations of great importance linked to a certain set of events in her childhood. Thus, we could say, the complex latched on to the idea of the analyst, but if this had been insisted on in the treatment, it might have closed the door to the further associations. Presumably the unsettling of parts of the unconscious complex produced the readiness for transference which manifested itself in the choice of the household product. As the psyche becomes the site of a tension due to the work of analysis, resistance takes on the form of the creation of sentiments which mask their real sources. Many instances of the sudden emergence of a strange idea or an unexpected emotion involve the same preliminaries: something has been happening which creates a state of tension, and thus a portion of the complex will be on the lookout for something to latch on to. In the context of love relations, the choice of lover may thus have little to do with their person: they might have to embody certain details that matter, but ultimately they also have to be in the right place at the right time. That's why it is sometimes possible to say that a man or a woman is going to fall in love, that they are on the lookout, even if no partner is immediately there on the horizon. What's there first is a readiness, generated by a particular form of unease, the unsettling of an unconscious complex or, to put it another way, the experience of a set of significant disappointments.

Reik took up the Freudian argument to try to explain this readiness to fall in love. Something must happen, he says, to produce a state of dissatisfaction in ourselves, the equivalent of the state of tension that will be artificially produced in an analysis. We are aware of something lacking from ourselves, something that is missing, a gap, perhaps, between ourselves and some ideal. This introduction of a tension sets up the initial condition, which can be felt as nostalgia, restlessness or discontent. But when we then encounter a person who seems to embody those traits which we have deemed lacking from ourselves, the first reaction is not love but envy. Although we can be angry with an inferior, we can only hate someone in a superior position, someone who has something we don't, who has some power over us. And now the key turning point of the process of falling in love takes place, the moment when the decision is made unconsciously to make this envy pass into love – or to consolidate itself as hate.

Reik tells a charming and no doubt idealised story here. The philosopher Mendelssohn, a small and hunchbacked man, fell in love with the daughter of a noble merchant on a visit to Hamburg, a woman who had many qualities but not a hunchback. After a stay of some weeks, he visited the girl's father at his office and asked him what she had said about him. The father replied, 'Well, you are a philosopher and a wise man: you will not take it amiss. The child said that she got frightened when she saw you, because . . .' and then he paused. 'Because I am a hunchback,' said the philosopher. The merchant nodded. Mendelssohn requested a last visit to bid her farewell, and found her busy with needlework. She avoided his eyes as he spoke to her, but he led the conversation carefully to the theme of marriage. She asked him whether he too believed that marriages were made in heaven. 'Certainly,' he said, 'and something quite unusual happened to me. As you know, they call out in heaven at the birth of a child, "This one and that one will get this and that girl for a wife." When I was born, my future wife was also thus announced, but it was added, "She will, alas, have a terrible hump on her back." I shouted, "Oh, God, Lord, a girl who is hunchbacked will very easily become bitter and hard. A girl should be beautiful. Good Lord, give the hump to me and let her be handsome and well formed."' So said the philosopher, and the girl, deeply moved, stretched out her hand to him and became his faithful and loving wife. This tender story evokes the Renaissance idea of the exchange of places in love, in which beloved becomes lover, and shows how the presence of a trait which is lacking – in this case, the hunchback – operates as the principle of transformation in a love story.

The envy that Reik privileges is absent from this tale, but, if we accepted his argument, it would have been present at the encounter with the woman who had what the philosopher lacked. This is not, in fact, such a new idea. The medieval writer Richard of St Victor, for example, held that hate is inseparable from the extreme of both carnal and spiritual love. Whatever happens, the envy is there at the start: love, if it is to emerge, will always have a form of hatred as its foundation, and this is perhaps why if love often takes a long time to develop it can turn so swiftly into hate. The usual argument here is to explain such reversals as due simply to oversensitiveness: vindictiveness in couples is so powerful since if love is all about self-esteem, the tiniest slight will throw the lover back onto their old insecurities. But the tiny slight may also be exactly what the lover waits for: it is sought in order to allow the envy and hatred to emerge. If a man returns home after squandering some of the precious family income on the horses, he might be especially keen to reproach his wife for some trivial domestic 'error', but this sort of local reversal of blame is only the tip of the iceberg. Many people are continually on the lookout for something in their partner's behaviour which can be used as an opportunity for attack, some little gesture or careless phrase which can then take on the enormity of an insult or aggression. In such cases, one could speak of a readiness not just to fall in love but to continue hating. Which emerges once again at precisely those moments when it shouldn't: for example, when the loved one has got a cold. Instead of compassionate concern, what one finds here so often is just its opposite, a sort of vengeful spite as if it were entirely the partner's fault that they had fallen ill. The same concern is frequent in the family: although they 'know better', children often feel that the parent is to blame for being ill, just as a parent may grudge the child with the same reproach. How can this be explained?

One idea, though certainly not the only one, is linked to a question posed by female homosexuality. If Freudian daughters like their dads and even expect one day to receive a child from them, there is the problem of why it is that some women, who have the greatest love for their fathers, turn not to men but to other women. The simple explanation is that if only one man counts, the others aren't worth anything. Also, if the love from the father proves discontinuous – for example, if he gives the baby to someone else – the daughter might try to demonstrate what a real love is by loving a woman with great devotion. The idea being, 'This is how a woman ought to be loved.' She will give to another woman what she did not receive herself from the father, thus giving what she hasn't got. Lacan nuanced these ideas with the remark that a woman who loves women may be someone who refuses to accept the castration of men. Now, to make some sense of this idea one can start with the Freudian observation that a daughter may have a great love for the father but the key is to see that a father is a complicated set of things, not just one real live flesh and blood object. What a girl might love is not the real man but the idea of the father, which is rather different. After all, real fathers measure up or fail to measure up according to certain ideas of what a father is. There are some women who do not wish to accept that this ideal is a broken one, that man suffers castration, that he is lacking something. They hate the admission from a man that he is dependent on them, whereas for other women this admission is actively pursued. When the film-maker Carol Reed told Daphne du Maurier that he couldn't do without her, it was a real turn-off. In classical Freudian terms, the idea of castration here is woven into the oedipal story: the man must be made to have something, since if he did not, how could the girl receive anything from him?

Although it would be quite correct to assume that many daughters have an affection for their fathers, we can remember here that Freud would modify his argument to claim that the first great commitment for both sexes is to the mother. The father, in this sense, acts as a kind of rescue station, and his ideal as someone having something can therefore be magnified. But beyond this commitment to the idea of a man is a prior commitment to a woman, and perhaps this offers a clue to the strange hostility to the father that a daughter will often show on the death of her mother and also the striking way in which women tend to apologise for their negative associations about their mothers in analysis. Whereas many men speak with some satisfaction about their hostility towards the mother and also the father, women frequently punctuate their speech with remarks like 'It wasn't really that bad' or express a conscious sense of guilt for disparaging the mother's image. In Freudian terms, it's as if the initial commitment of the Oedipus complex is present beneath the many associations which articulate the further, secondary, commitment to the father.

Now, if Freudian daughters turn first of all from their mothers to their fathers in order to receive something, the commitment to a man who is not lacking will take on a sense as the pivot of this transfer: otherwise, how could she leave the universe of the mother? The man only makes sense here if he has something. The contrast would be between those women with a passionate commitment to the man who has escaped and those who search, on the contrary, for a man marked by weakness, one who most certainly does not have something. Hence the fascination of a modern figure like Chris Patten – defined precisely by what he had to give up, he takes on the special quality of being the man who lost Hong Kong. Some women, indeed, are drawn to men who seem to have 'nothing to lose', since they have lost everything already, their job, their wife, their money and so on. The obvious explanation here would be that, with nothing to lose, the woman can find in the man an image of herself. More interesting, perhaps, would be to argue that if the man lacks nothing, in becoming what causes his desire, a woman can produce a lack in the man and then function herself as the cause of this lack. She becomes, as it were, the organ without which he cannot function. Hence the way in which Rebecca West would be so touched by H. G. Wells' descriptions of her absence: it was like 'the feeling of suddenly missing a limb', he said, a sentence which was guaranteed in its effects. When Ovid generously gave his advice to seducers, he recommended that they conceal any premeditated plan from the partner, so as to give to the sexual encounter the flavour of something entirely new and self-created. The excitement would be situated, he guessed, in the idea that each party is causing what the other feels, and it is true that for some women there is a great satisfaction in knowing that they are able, even with some trivial gesture, to excite a man sexually. A woman spoke of her difficulties in leaving a man whose humours most certainly contradicted her own, yet felt bound to him by the satisfaction she felt in knowing that she could arouse him by having the belt of her dressing gown tightly tied. It was this action on the man that she could not give up. Being in the place of the cause here may also shed light on why it is that a woman may begin a relation with a man, only to discard him after the first night they spend together: the subsequent move to the next man in the series articulates the ongoing process of investigating whether a man's desire can be aroused: whether, that is, she is in the place of the cause or not.

Now, when a man gets sick, this might be construed as a sign of weakness. And hence the way it may produce special tenderness in some women. But if, for others, what matters is to refuse the idea of castration in a man, the last thing such a woman might want is to see him incapacitated. If the man is ill, she becomes furious, rather than loving, a constant which also illuminates the old problem of so-called female masochism. Despite Lacan's polemic against the use of this term, it often emerges in veiled form in analytic literature. A classic example would be someone like Florence Nightingale, devoting her energies to helping wounded and sick men. But this is quite false: if one wishes to employ the term 'masochism' in a purely descriptive way here, a masochistic woman is not one who spends all her time looking after the sick, but one who, when a man is sick, won't have it. In other words, so great is her attachment to the idea of man as not lacking something, that when he actually displays his weakness in some form, she turns away in fury. When Helene Deutsch said that masochism was the strongest of all forms of love, it was perhaps in this sense: the commitment which is so much more powerful than the others is to this idea of a man as not lacking. Which makes of the forever potent man a figure of feminine rather than masculine fantasy, as Lacan once suggested. To elaborate this theme, one would have to explore the figure of the mother concealed beneath this idea of the man, but it shows nonetheless how the accentuations of having and not having have vigorous effects on the passions.

This may be linked to the motif of rescue we discussed in the last chapter. To love the wounded man is to dedicate oneself to the man's castration, but there is also the possibility, in refusing it, of simply denying that the man is wounded. The perfect test case here is that of a man surrounded by women who has exerted a special fascination for so many years: Branwell Brontë. This miserable youth attracts people in a very strange way, and when his merits and faults are being debated it is quickly evident from the hardiness of polemic that personal prejudices are at stake. While the sisters wrote their books, Branwell did some writing and painting himself, until he wore himself out with drink, drugs and perhaps an affair with one Mrs Robinson. Branwell has proved fascinating for several reasons: the only male in a group of female siblings, where they excelled, he failed. In his dedication to drink and drugs, he provides an early example of the teen hero mystique, the misunderstood man who lacks a sensible woman to look after him. He incarnates a sort of failure of will, resolute in his determination to be a failure for his father. As Charlotte understated it: 'Branwell was his father's and his sisters' pride and hope in boyhood, but since manhood the case has been otherwise.' And yet, so powerful was Branwell's image that it was only once he had died that all the other sisters could die in their turn. Charlotte, Emily and Anne were taken sick and the latter two sisters would both die within a year. In the famous National Gallery portrait of the three sisters, it is his ghostly image that forms the backdrop for their figures. Although he seems to become excluded from their collaborations and gossip after the sisters' first book of poems, his presence was still strong enough to signal their death. Whereas many female commentators and Brontë scholars have no intention of saving Branwell, others endeavour to demonstrate the merit of his compositions, to get him out of trouble, and, like Daphne du Maurier, who wrote a book about him, to show that he possessed more than he lacked. Filling in the endless biographical gaps with her own imagination, she muses on how proud he must have been to have a penis, and how he was supremely attached to his father. When she watched Margaret Drabble's television programme about the Brontës, she was livid to hear that Branwell didn't do much except drink at the Black Bull. For du Maurier, he had to be saved from castration at all costs, perhaps because, if she had always adored the image of the 'son' herself, if he could escape castration, then so could she.

We have seen how falling in love will have several conditions: a readiness caused by some discontent, the transformation of hatred and the priority of details. The symmetry of beginning and ending can be seen clearly with all of these features: the uneasiness after a love relation, the re-emergence of hatred and the isolation of those little things that you once loved which have now become thorns. Considering the first two of these factors, Reik concluded that the touchstone of love is not the absence of hostility or cruelty, present in every relationship, but rather of envy and greediness, even if these latter must be there at the start. Although this formulation of the development of love is open to criticism from a psychoanalytic perspective, and the idea of the absence of envy and greediness seems a touch idealistic, the interest of Reik's argument lies in the motif of the decision: something will decide the passage of envy and hatred into love. Goethe's remark, 'There are no means of safety against the superior qualities of another person but to love him', takes on all its value here. It provides, in fact, a definition of what it means to be a man. Freud had argued in one of his last papers that the stumbling block in the analysis of men was their difficulty in assuming a passive position in relation to another man, of accepting or not accepting their subordination. A man could thus be defined as someone who is able to admire other men. This seems too simple, but it can be tested by contrasting those men who are forever idealising other men, a situation which usually doesn't last too long, and those men who, when facing their counterparts, have no response but hatred and derision. Admiration and respect are situated in between these alternatives and, as anyone can verify, they are not the commonest of male attitudes.

These traits, it's true, are not usually a part of the popular vision of what's masculine, with its focus on competition and strength. But competition is often only a surface phenomenon, and it is equally common to find its contrary, an avoidance of competition in those men, for example, who are always waiting for the authorisation of their actions. Freud spoke about rivalry in the relation of sibling to sibling, but added that one could opt instead for an early retirement. If one child is especially gifted at music, the other child may either decide to compete or to retire in their favour, suddenly 'becoming' untalented and choosing another field of interest. Which would explain the often baffling 'failures' of school children in a subject which they had once excelled in. When Robertson and Hume were both engaged in their histories, Robertson abdicated his study lest it should injure the plans of Hume. This sort of early retirement avoids conflict, but that does not mean that the conflict goes away. Instead, as Lacan points out, the subject may spend their whole life waiting in the shadows for the death of the opponent, forever anticipating the events in the future which will change their life and which, by necessity, will have no place but the future. Hence the well-known fact that the man who is the most tortured by hostile and destructive thoughts is often the same man who will most scrupulously avoid conflict. If some people pursue a noisy revenge against the one they hate, others will take revenge on themselves for not having pursued anything: as Reik observed, they never forgive themselves for the harm they have failed to do to others.

This logic of love and hate provides a solution to the old problem of why Romeo and Juliet didn't just take off together, avoiding all the feuding in Verona. Rather than seeing their love as an impassioned defiance of the feud between Capulets and Montagues, Reik pointed out that perhaps it was not entirely a matter of chance that they were to fall in love. As Juliet says on learning the identity of her Romeo, 'My only love sprung from my only hate.' Beneath their romance lies the real hatred of the two families, and it is this hostility which ultimately drives them to their death. Hatred produced their love rather than providing its obstacle, a twist which would explain their strange love which seems to crystallise after just one short and vacuous meeting. It comes not from the particulars of the person, but from the battle of the families. Thus the fate of the lovers at the end of the play reflects the opening itself, where servants and nephews of the two families aggress each other quite openly. Romeo is to Juliet what Laura was to Petrarch, a 'beloved enemy', where it is the enemy that comes first, and not the beloved.

This play poses another important question about love. In the first act, Romeo is speaking about his romantic problems, and then says immediately, 'Where shall we dine?' This is very strange. If someone is in love, they tend to have appetite problems, and this to such an extent that if someone consistently neglects their food, a state of love is often diagnosed. The last thing the lovesick think of is a huge meal. The appetite is so finely tuned here to desire that in a story like *Wuthering Heights*, every time anything at all happens in the entire book, someone stops eating. In a sense, to say that it is a novel about love is no different from saying it is a novel about people stopping eating. Even in a time well before the 'invention' of romantic love, Ovid's Echo is still no longer able to eat once her pining for Narcissus sets in. And when Narcissus falls for his own image, he gets the same symptom, until he eventually starves to death. But this in itself is mysterious. Love, after all, is supposed to involve incorporating one's partner, becoming one with them, and the many expressions in the world's languages ('I'll eat you up' etc.) reiterate this. The lover might therefore be expected to have a big appetite but this is hardly the case. If we remember Freud's notion of a 'readiness' here, we might conjecture that Romeo's appetite is linked less to love than to a readiness to love. The friar is amazed, later in the play, that Romeo could abandon his initial love for Rosalie so swiftly for Juliet. Juliet, rather than serving as the cause for the loss of appetite, is the person who comes into the place of the large meal. That may be why, once he loves her, food becomes less important.

It is thus a woman who stops Romeo from eating, a formula which we find in the Vandal epic of the waning of Perdica. This studious young man is about to leave Athens for his home, when he neglects for some reason to sacrifice to Venus and Cupid. He is visited, in consequence, by a dream image which captivates him, causing him to fall in love and to reject all form of nourishment. The only problem here is that the dream image is that of the young man's mother. When the latter summons a doctor, the medic discovers that his pulse increases whenever she enters the room, and putting two and two together, he does the sensible thing and resigns the case. If we look to this story for a clue to the eating disorder, the obstacle to eating may be the same as the obstacle which gives the law of the prohibition of incest. From this perspective, food is not incorporated because of its link to the mother. It is not just because the lover has too much on his mind to think about taking care of his diet, but because this too much is connected to the forbidden figure of the mother, and thus what's too much has to be converted into what's too little. The ban on the mother becomes the prohibition on eating. This theory is cute, but unconvincing. All it really demonstrates is something agreed on by the most diverse authorities: that there is a special relation between food and love.

Most modern researchers will agree that this is a key factor in the two major eating disorders, anorexia and bulimia, but what is so often overlooked is the fact that these difficulties may have little in common. Although their manifest symptoms are often found in a rhythmic relationship, that doesn't mean that they are the same thing. Rather than seeing a continuum which stretches from the one to the other, it is sometimes more accurate to separate them, a division which is reflected in the distribution of these conditions in early childhood: whereas it is quite common to find infantile anorexias in pre-school age children, bulimia is extremely rare. Why might this be the case? The link of food and love is a a good place to start. As Lacan showed, the infant's first appeals for nourishment will have unexpected and inevitable consequences: asking puts the mother in the powerful position of the one who can respond or not respond, and what is asked for thus becomes secondary to the question of how the other shows their love. If the mother replies, it's a sign: it is not the food object as such that matters, but whether there is a reply or not. Which explains the continuous demands of children which go well beyond the limits of biological nourishment. Food thus becomes a sign of something else, and the vicissitudes of the child's relation to food will take on a meaning within this framework. The French philosopher Léon Brunschwicg spoke of the decisive moment in his life when he liberated himself from the religion of his parents: it was a time of fasting, so to signal his separation he made up his mind to have something to eat. But this might be construed, he feared, as simply the conquest of his appetite over his principles, so to demonstrate the contrary he chose to eat just one single bean. The bean, for Brunschwicg, was a sign, not simply a morsel to be devoured, and the less of it there was, the more the dimension of signs, the symbolic refusal, could be stressed.

Reik tells the story of a patient who complains of his oscillation from apathy to manic states, from feeling like a sinner to feeling elevated and saintly, and who switched with regularity from his depressions to a sharp self-mockery. He would deprive himself of food in his moods of atonement and go on a binge of eating when his self-accusations quietened down. One Sunday morning, he arrives at the home of his family, ready to make peace for a change with his father and stepmother. When he enters the living room, unannounced, he sees among the other things laid out on the breakfast table a large coffee cake. As his relatives continue chatting in the next room, unaware of his arrival, he overhears some unfavourable remarks about himself. Seized by a sudden rage, he takes the coffee cake that had been destined for the family gathering, tiptoes to the door and leaves in silence. As he hurries home through the streets, he eats the whole cake in an attack of voracious fury. Now, how can this passionate appetite be understood?

From one perspective, it represents simply an attack on the relatives, displaced to the cake: the hostility has reverted to its original oral form, which supposes a devouring with no mercy. More interesting is the idea of the balance between demands and the objects associated with needs. When someone is frustrated in love, there is a form of compensation at the level of need, a possibility introduced by the original contrast between the signifying dimension of the relation to the mother, her power to respond or not respond, and the child's relation to the breast as an object of satisfaction. As the mother fails to respond to the child who calls her, he may fix himself to the breast. The crucial point here, as Lacan argued, is in the balance between these two dimensions: the breast is not an original primary object, but takes on its value *as* a primary object due to the symbolic background in which the child relates to it. It wouldn't function as an object of satisfaction to compensate the child if there wasn't the prior problem of the symbolic object, the object as a sign of something else. Later on, other elements may be put into this place of the object of satisfaction, but always responding to some hurt or frustration played out at another level.

The story of the coffee cake illustrates this nicely, as the act of devouring follows the overhearing of a slight, and it also shows how there is more than one dimension to the object that is consumed. The patient had entered unannounced, like a ghost, yet although he leaves without revealing his presence, he has nonetheless left a calling card: the absence of the cake. There are thus two sides to the story: on the one hand, the absence of the cake from the family table, and on the other the presence of the cake in the frantic act of devouring. It is not simply a question of focusing on the coffee cake as an oral object, as something to be devoured, but also as a sign. More precisely, the sign is the absence of the coffee cake, since it is this which takes on the value of a footprint in the home he has left so silently. Like Brunschwicg's single bean, it may be both an object that is swallowed *and* linked to the register of signs, but if so, what exactly does it stand for? According to one psychoanalytic conception, it may represent a person, a loved or hated relative, or alternatively a part of the body like the breast. We might remember here that cannibals only eat the ones they love and respect. When the great English philosopher John McTaggart Ellis McTaggart was a child, he had been regaled with tales of indigenous cannibalism, yet what particularly fascinated him was the idea that the qualities of one person could be transfused into another by eating. His memories of this time converge on the scene of walking along the top of a garden wall, telling his mother how he intended eating her for his supper. Luckily, McTaggart's modernity saved him from the old problem of what happens if you eat your mother: if one body absorbs another, what's supposed to happen at Last

Judgement when resurrection occurs? Cannibals are in a tricky situation here. If McTaggart had subscribed to the theory of an Athenagoras, according to which human flesh could not genuinely absorb human flesh, cannibals would always be getting thinner, and so being lean would just mean that one had been eating the wrong things.

A two and a half year old boy I worked with had stopped eating. In his articulation of his worries, it became clear that there was a problem with eating since, for this child, to eat and to be eaten were one and the same thing. Hence his terror at mealtimes: confronted with his plate, it was his own existence that was at stake. Shortly after this eating difficulty set in, he developed a particular fascination with a children's book, telling the story of a gang of small animals trying to evade a larger predator bent on devouring them. At the end of the story the predator is banished by a storm. The predator in question was linked, by a particular detail, to the boy's mother, and, reading the story through with him, instead of the name of this animal, I said the word 'mother' instead. Which produced two very interesting results. Firstly, as he became able to eat once more, he began to make repeated references to a storm, even though the weather was clement. The storm was not a word referring to a change in the weather, but a representation, a signifier of what took the place of the mother's devouring impulses. And, as a linguistic term introduced into the child's terrors, it had a mediating function, allowing him to construct scenarios and new games around the motif of the storm. Secondly, a new piece of material emerged now for the first time. He spoke of his brother, and said several times 'I'm dying of hunger', until this sentence became transformed into 'I'm dying of Jonathan', the name of the new sibling. The brother posed the question, with all its urgency, of the desire of the mother, of what the mother wanted, which, due to the new arrival, was no longer identical with the first son. Into the place of this question of what value he had for the mother came the latter's devouring powers and the only solution seemed: to become eaten.

Children, oddly enough, think that animal and human shaped biscuits are fun to eat. Although this shows us man's propensities for devouring those closest to him, there is also the fact that animals and humans mean something, they have resonances as mythic beings: in other words, they tell stories. If an animal can tell a story, to eat one is to eat a story. Which is one definition of what becoming human is all about. As the New Testament says, man swallows the Word, which gives him life. In some cultures, if someone is unwell, a passage from a religious writing is inscribed inside an earthen bowl which is then filled with water. As it is stirred around, the writing is worked off, and the patient drinks the solution, thus infusing the sacred words. To get better, it is the word which must be ingested, just as for McTaggart eating was a question of incorporating the qualities of the thing eaten. The importance of animals here is not difficult to guess: an animal may be a mythic creature and a totemic one, but it is ultimately a creature of the Word. As a totem, an animal matters less as what it is – if you belong to a group with the totem animal of the bear, that doesn't mean that you are strong and grizzly – than as the marker of difference – you can't get married to someone of the same totem, for example.

The animal functions as a symbolic element, to organise and distribute certain structures. Swallowing an animal may thus be one example among others of an activity which consists of swallowing the word, a symbolic element. But even for humans, totems do not just come naturally: they are artefacts which matter precisely because of their artificiality. Lacan focused on this feature in his discussion of infantile phobia, arguing that what mattered about the object of the phobia was its symbolic character. If the father is first and foremost a symbolic function different from the real biological man, then in order to incarnate this function, the best way might be with something that is obviously artificial, something that is clearly marked off from 'nature'. That civilisation is forever sensitive to this symbolic separation is made clear in Japanese restaurants. The food might be raw, but the sushi always comes with a useless piece of plastic greenery, to remind us that we are never really in the realm of 'nature' without the presence of something artificial. A heraldic animal embodies this artificiality very well, since it has its value as a symbolic, organising element and is linked to a web of myths and stories which give it even greater symbolic density. Children develop animal phobias often at a particular time: when the symbolic side of paternity is not being transmitted in a family for some reason, the child can try to make it emerge in the form of the totem animal he or she is afraid of. When the function of the father is required to separate mother from child, and the real father can't manage to do this properly, a new element is introduced into the family: the name of the animal which the child continually refers to. This establishes new organising principles, as it determines where the child can go or not go, what can be done and not done and so on. And, if it works, a minimum of symbolic functioning is reinforced and the phobia can then make its spontaneous disappearance, as it often does. Perhaps it is the attachment to the totemic aspect of the animal that explains the amazing behaviour of military staff during the First World War: whatever the experts had to report, getting rid of the horse in favour of the tank was clearly one of the army's most difficult decisions and it was made only too late, after many lives had been lost. Which shows the difficulty in getting rid of an insignia, a mythic image which has mattered for centuries.

❦

If there may be several reasons for incorporating food, there is still the question of why it is sometimes necessary to expel it so quickly. A middle-aged woman complained of her urgent devouring of sweets, followed by vomiting in conditions of secrecy. After some time a scene was recalled from childhood in which she was whispering with a cousin about sex and reproduction. The cousin informed her that a liquid is secreted from Daddy's willy when he is alone with Mum, which is like melted sugar. After the recall of this scene, the particular moments when she would binge revealed a logic. They would invariably occur after some disappointment from a man, either in a love relation or simply a slight when she was talking with her father or brother on the telephone. Now, this might seem to explain the bulimic trait: the incorporating of sweets was derived from the desire to possess the sugary solution, and the secrecy of the binge reflected the forbidden nature of the act itself. Like the medieval nuns forbidden from taking endless communion in an effort to consume in the wafer as much of the Christ as possible, the devouring was aimed at something beyond the reality of the sweet. But how, then, can the expulsion of the food, the vomiting up, be accounted for?

One interpretation would link the sequence 'to incorporate – to vomit' with the fantasy of childbirth, being played out here at an imaginary level. Something is ingested and then expelled, with the bodily location being shifted from down below – the genitals – to up above – the mouth. This might seem to be supported by the clinical example we just discussed, since the food devoured was clearly linked to the idea of the phallus, and it would perhaps explain the severe vomiting which accompanies some pregnancies. Medicine has not yet found a good explanation for the vicissitudes that characterise this fact, and the curious observation has been made that women who vomit frequently during their pregnancy seem to have a lower risk of miscarriage. I have not seen any convincing evidence for this claim and in fact certain factors would suggest quite the opposite, but the point to be made is that although one may give a 'biological' explanation for vomiting, it is clear that how much or how little a pregnant woman vomits is often linked to psychic factors. The problem in our example is the displacement from below to above, as if the genital region has been cancelled out. A clinical vignette from the case of a woman suffering from a variety of symptoms linked to 'imagined' pregnancies gives us a clue here. She first seeks help after a series of disastrous relationships. She is aware that she has what she calls a 'daddy complex', yet the logic of the bonds and the effects of her attachment are still obscure. One of the first things she reports is that during a recent fling with a man whose religion forbade him to eat pig, she had experienced a craving for pork chops. Soon, she has a dream which takes place in the official residence of her father. She is with her elder sister in the father's bed, and says to the sibling, 'Wake up! We've got to pay the landlord and the landlord's mother has called to say that he is dead.' The sister replies that she knows he's not dead, since they were going to pay him. To which the dreamer replies 'No! Let me sleep. I am giving a funeral to my sex.' A number of pink flowers are growing from her genitals which she recognises as bougainvillaeas. She wakes up with the sentence echoing in her head, 'This is the dream of the death of my sex' and a feeling of amazing serenity and contentment.

Now, what can this clinical material tell us about the problems we have been discussing? First of all, the location of the dream. It takes place in the official and not the family home of the father, indicating a reference to his symbolic status: it is the home of a man with an official function. Next, it turns out that the pink flowers, the bougainvillaeas, are the only plant that the father, a keen gardener, refuses to have anywhere in sight. He forbids anyone to plant them due to a singular and unexplained aversion. A symmetry with the pork chop craving emerges here: both the chop and the flowers are forbidden objects for those concerned, and in each case she assumes them, in the first by eating, in the second by the site of their cultivation. These objects are thus both excluded ones, they have a special role in the field of desire as indicating what is different, what is outside and prohibited. The link with her genitals gives them the value of the phallus, not simply as a real organ but as the symbol of desire, as the associations with the two men reveal: they indicate what is out of reach. But what about the sentence, 'This is the dream of the death of my sex'? If we link the dream material with the problems of displacement we have been discussing, the sex becomes cancelled out with the appearance of the flowers. The question of the dead landlord evokes that of the dead father, a death which is shifted to her own sex, suggesting that her sex now migrates to a new site. The identificatory link with the father which is being expressed here is what entails the shift from below to above, and the oral cravings thus follow from the death of her sex. If we take the example seriously, it nuances the earlier thesis about the fantasies of pregnancy: pregnancy does not just involve the birth of a baby, but refers to the phallus which will take on the form of the child. Eating and desire thus enjoy a special relationship, and shed light on the way in which a disappointment in love can trigger both a renewed passion for food or an abstinence.

One might note here that people don't just eat food, they

make promises about it. Being true to a diet is a very serious business, and it raises the question of whether it is possible to do so given the fact that a diet is an order, a linguistic set of rules, which is introduced to structure the life of the dieter. Possibly, it falls within the same series as the many plans and rules for future life that adolescent girls sometimes formulate and impose on themselves. If it is a matter of the greatest importance for many women to demonstrate that they are not identical with a set of rules, that they are, as it were, different from their diet, it may be unwise to suppose that a diet is something to be true to. A cookery book is more exciting than a book on how to diet since it contains many different possibilities, without imposing one formula on the reader. Indeed, there may even be a particular delight in not following a recipe to the letter, by innovating, adding and altering. What this shows is that to understand something of the complicated relations a woman may have with a diet, one has to realise that it is not just a question of food, but of language, a relation to a set of instructions. The critic Julie Burchill once pointed out that whereas young people used to have passionate commitments to causes outside the body (Vietnam, education etc.), today these causes have moved inward: what really matters to such a large percentage of the population is what they are eating, what's going on inside rather than outside their stomachs. But the more concern there is with matters of diet, the more problematic the relation to the cause becomes due to the difficulties of remaining true to it. There is even a satisfaction in not following the rules here, which might give a clue as to why people who frequent health food stores always look so unhealthy. The solution here might be simple: to write cookery books where in the place of each recipe is a diet that is different from the others.

These ideas complicate the standard argument that people

eat in order to fill up a gap, as they indicate the complexities of both the use and the meaning of gaps. Some restaurants have made their fortune with a policy of 'All you can eat' and the behaviour of their habitués is often instructive. Many diners are attracted by the offer, but will eat no more than anyone else: in fact, they may well eat less. Others will eat more, but their consumption extends much further than their natural appetite. The idea of outdoing the restaurateur becomes privileged over the question of their own health, so that the 'All you can eat' becomes less a possibility than an imperative. Hence the prudent introduction of small-scale salad bowls. For others, the offer has the modest function of reassurance: that supplies are there, just in case. But the real problem of culinary generosity is that there is no such thing as 'All you can eat'. If there is an emptiness, a vacuum of desire, at the heart of each man and each woman, no real object can fill it. What matters is keeping desire going, maintaining the dimension of the empty space and dreaming about what might respond to it, which on a global level might be 'Mr Right' and on a local level might be a Four Seasons pizza.

The only people who are genuinely concerned with the 'All you can eat' policy are mothers, as they are perpetually alert to the dangerous prospects of their babies exploring each new object by inserting it into the mouth. This is no doubt the real reason why people open their mouths when surprised: just as the child tests each new object in its environment by moving it towards the mouth, so as adults, when we witness something unexpected or strange, we repeat the same gesture. If putting an object into one's mouth counts as filling a gap, we need to turn our attention to what happens a bit later on, and how boys and girls, and men and women, relate to the absences and gaps which both punctuate and structure their existence.

Five

In *Brief Encounter*, the lovers arrange to meet each other in the gap between trains. For men, this in-betweenness is a condition which could be elevated to the status of a paradigm: that's the place where they fall in love. In modern cities, stations are the privileged place for glimpsing someone who might have made your life different. The face on the passing train or the figure going down the escalator while you're going up will take on a special value, a brilliance linked to being in between, fleeting, evoking the dimension of loss and what escapes us. But why should this condition matter so much? To understand its logic, we need to know more about railways, and, more precisely, about the meaning of a railway timetable.

The linguist Ferdinand de Saussure used the idea of the railway timetable as an illustration of what a language is and how it is organised. Each element in a system will take on its value owing to its difference from the other elements. The 10 o'clock train can arrive at 10.15, but it is still the 10 o'clock train due to its difference from the 10.30 and the 9.30 train. The carriages can be blue on one day and red the next, but it will still be the 10.30 train owing to its difference from the others. The timetable is like a language since its values are given by differences, just as each word in a language will take on its value by being different from other words. The implication of this idea for an understanding of the sexes is capital, even if the linguistic theory itself is rather limited. If elements take on their value owing to their difference from each other, a language must be made up of a set of elements with gaps in between. If the railway timetable only has one train, it isn't much of a timetable, just as if all the trains come at the same time one would get confused. As discrete elements, there's a gap in between, and this in-betweenness is what matters to men and women, but in different ways.

Winnicott had the intuition that in-betweenness was a key concept in psychoanalytic theory, but it was Lacan who linked it with the structure of language. To put it simply, what matters to human beings are things that are not entirely subsumed in speaking, things that are evoked, enigmatic and not understood. Our own being can never be made identical with words, and hence the logical place for all these questions is not in words but in between words. Whereas a woman may do her best to demonstrate that in-betweenness matters, that this gap which separates our being and words exists, a man is more likely to try to obscure it, to cover it over and erase it. If a woman can be late for a train, a man is quite likely to have memorised the timetable in its entirety, just as men like lists of facts, bits of information to be stuck onto the world. The philosopher Kant never ventured outside his home town of Königsberg, yet he was proud of his large collection of atlases. What he didn't know at the level of tourism, he knew with the literature of travel, yet this might have been simply a practical fidelity to his own thesis that sense experience is always structured by pre-existing ideas in the first place. Similarly, it has been pointed out that when a woman says, 'Let's talk,' men tend to see this as the first moment of criticism rather than conversation. But when some men *want* to talk, and to continue talking with the compulsive honesty we noted earlier on, this may be less the sign of an unveiling of their being than just its opposite: once again, the effort to make everything a part of speech, to assimilate an alterity to a language. This may be contrasted with the old association of women and riddles: a riddle is a piece of language, and to solve it, an object has to be identified which fits the description. To remain a riddle is to remain an unsolved riddle, and hence the requirement that there is *not* a match between the object and the description. But men tend to want the match. It is much more likely to find a man boring everyone at a dinner party with displays of information, keen not only to broadcast titbits but to obstruct any other knowledge which he cannot impart himself. This kind of relation to knowledge must have its reasons: why is it so important for some men to know everything, and to contract the wonders of the universe to a list of facts?

Getting rid of gaps for a man means to keep working mentally, to immerse himself as much as possible in the verbal chains of thinking. The more thoughts there are, the more the gaps can be deferred. The more lists made and the longer and more exhaustive they are, the more likely, it seems, that nothing will be left out. The first but by no means the only problem here is that in writing a list, one thing always gets left out: the time you waste in writing it. The busy and industrious philosopher Leibniz was a man who took pride in always thinking and calculating. He noted down his ideas on paper wherever he was, then put aside the drafts without reading them through again, so urgent was the necessity of the next transcription. The philosopher's thesis that language is the bridge between mind and matter and that no thought could be separated from some material trace was no doubt how he explained this mountain of jottings to those it perplexed. And as the Leibniz scholar Allison Coudert notes, it was the very accumulation of these jottings that hindered him from finding the ones he needed to, and he thus had to start all over again, illustrating how the thought machine always produces an effect of loss at some level. It was his thinking that provided the obstacle to his thinking, and it was this obstacle which set him thinking all over again.

Thinking for men often takes the form of calculating or counting, with the idea that numbers can play the same role as words in warding off a gap. When the composer Anton von Brückner took a train from Vienna, it stopped for a few minutes in the countryside, and in that time he counted the windows of a house he could see from the train window. But as the train moved on, he began to wonder if he had counted right, and his wondering became an anxiety. He got off the train at the next stop and walked all the way back to the house to make sure he had counted correctly, despite the inconvenience this supplied to his musical career. In the place of the gap in the train journey, the momentary pause, he put thinking, which in this case took the form of counting. A clue to this strange behaviour is found in another anecdote told of the musician, his tendency to follow young ladies in order to make sure he had counted correctly the beads on their necklaces. In other words, assuming a priority for young ladies over houses, what mattered for him was the problem of whether there was something he hadn't counted on a woman's body. The gap of castration thus becomes bound up with the compulsion to count, where both numbers and words are used to absorb what can never be ultimately taken up into the sponge of thinking. What wasn't there on the woman's body would become displaced to whatever it was that wasn't there in a house, a necklace and the gaps in his own mental arithmetic.

Loving may seem different from counting, but unfortunately they have much in common: the man who spends his whole day working with figures doesn't suddenly become a different person the moment he leaves work. And, as popular culture shows us, when a man does become a totally different person, you ought to stay indoors: he is more likely to turn into a werewolf than a kind and considerate lover. For many men, the continuity of counting and love life is quite conscious. They count their girlfriends or involve themselves in even more complex operations. When Boswell was weighing up the pros and cons of an evening out, he attempted a comparison of the cost of taking a lady out to dinner with that of visiting a prostitute, contracting the clap and then receiving medical care. Although the second alternative no doubt involved a more lengthy programme than the first, Boswell was keen to consider both of them, provided that the numbers matched. Behind this calculation is the effort to render something incalculable – introduced by the encounter with the opposite sex – into something calculable. What poses problems to thought becomes more thinkable once it is fitted into a numerical frame. It can even serve as the rationalisation for a move away from the opposite sex altogether. One patient described in the literature began his calculations with the idea that the stimuli leading to ejaculation in both coitus and masturbation are caused by continuous movement of certain parts of the penis, combined with pressure and friction. Now, to maintain the necessary movement, it is kinetically unimportant whether the foreskin moves and the rest of the penis remains at rest or, conversely, whether the foreskin remains at rest and the inside of the penis moves. In masturbation, the man is motionless and only the foreskin moves, but in coitus the man must move his whole body, assuming that the woman herself is motionless. If the foreskin weighs seven grams and the man's whole body weighs seventy kilos, then the kinetic energy required for the movement in coitus is ten thousand times as great as in masturbation. Thus anyone who prefers coitus to masturbation is like a man in the basement of a house who, instead of going upstairs, wants to have the whole house raised by the height of a storey in order to reach street level. The mathematical abilities of this man were no doubt unequal to those of his invention, yet his confusions demonstrate the way in which numbers are used in relation to the opposite sex. The psychoanalyst Karl Abraham had a case in which a woman was encouraged to participate, during coitus, in an auction sale of the bed, the bids increasing in proportion to the mounting excitement. And Balint reports a similar vignette in which a husband had to make bids for the sexual services of his wife during intercourse. The greater the satisfaction of the husband, so apparently the greater that of the wife, and the sum agreed upon could thus be increased, like at any good auction. But if a bid proved unrealistic, the auction would collapse, and the husband would procure no satisfaction from the sexual commerce. In this case, the counting is actually going on during the lovemaking, as its condition and not just its commentary. Sex is thus slipped into a framework guaranteed by numbers, and where the numbers go wrong, so does the sexual relation itself.

Although this sort of numerical, linguistic activity is characteristic of men, it is not absent in some women, showing that rather than speaking all the time about men and women, it would be more prudent to speak of different forms of sexual enjoyment, forms which although broadly distributed in the one sex may also be found in the other. A woman complained of difficulties in her love life and explained that in her frequent affairs with men, she would have to find out as quickly as possible how many women the man in question had already slept with. Once the figure had been obtained, she set herself the task of procuring the same number of orgasms with the man as there had been past girlfriends. What psychoanalysis added to this description was the question of whether, in her calculation, she included herself in the list of women. The fact that this was the case suggested that, adding herself to the series, she had chosen to situate herself, unconsciously, in the place of the man. Each of her orgasms thus marked one of his conquests: they were situated in a numerical frame which established her own symmetry with the man with whom she slept. The fact that she also counted her many boyfriends was unusual. Most women would have to think a little bit before such calculation, and it is more than likely that when they are asked to do this, it is a man who is doing the asking: the list is a reply to the man's inelegant question 'How many?' and *his own* concern to provide a framework. When Andie MacDowell reels off the list of men she has slept with from 1 to 33 in *Four Weddings and a Funeral*, it was Charles who asked her to do it. Which shows once again the tendencies of the man to situate the encounter of the sexes beneath the banner of number. When Don Juan counted his women, his counting was just as much a part of his sexual activity as his nights. Most people don't want to be a number, but to make other people numbers is just what matters to many men.

Could one say, in fact, that being in love just means counting to one, if all you do is think about a single person? This thesis is complicated by the fact that for one person to have a value, they are probably coming into the place of someone or something else. From a Freudian perspective, for example, a woman might be coming into the place of the lost mother of childhood. Or, in terms of the logic of gaps we have been discussing, into the place of a gap, an in-betweenness. In *Brief Encounter*, the woman is loved quite literally in the spaces between trains, and it is amazing how Alec and Laura never bother missing a train until right at the end of the film. Until then, all their encounters are tightly fitted into the schedule of the railway, as if the timetable were a condition, a part of the very fabric of their love affair: the gap in between is thus filled with the activity of loving and the image of a woman. But why should avoiding a gap be so important? And why do men always fall in love in between trains?

❦

As children, we are thrown into a world where others speak about us before we can speak back, where we are named and have our futures plotted out by those who bring us into the world, and before whom we are helpless. Promises are made in the name of a child both before it is born and before the time of speaking. As the Creed is read for the child at baptism, obligations are assumed for him which he or she cannot yet understand, yet which will be renewed each year. The medieval scholar Etienne Gilson remarked that the day comes when a choice has to be made: either to make in one's own name the promises once made for one by someone else, or formally to refuse to subscribe to them. In other words, it will become necessary to take on a place in the world of discourses around us. This is by no means a 'natural' process, since even our basic reactions will be determined by those of the parents. Anna Freud and her colleague Dorothy Burlingham worked with young children in London during the Blitz, and noted that children under the age of three did not have anxiety during the bombing raids until their mothers did. A child may thus 'learn' when to have certain feelings and how to make sense of the mother's behaviour, but there is still the margin beyond this where what the mother wants is terrifyingly unclear. We can have an idea what it is that those who care for us are demanding and what they are asking for, but there will always be elements which we do not understand and yet which concern us directly. We might have an idea of what mother is saying, but not about why she is saying it. That this generates the most profound unease may be seen from a domestic situation in the life of an adult: a woman would regularly explore the belongings of her husband when he was out of the house, not with any conscious idea of searching for evidence of an infidelity, but with the anxious expectancy that she might find something that would surprise, even terrify her. Although she could not say what this 'something' was, it incarnated the dimension of what was not known about the partner, the margin of his desire that was obscure and yet which seemed to concern her to the quick.

When two people are in the same place at the same time this is indeed one of the things that happens: the disturbing presence of something beyond the partner is felt, in this example taking on the form of the expectancy of finding some awful secret. Indeed, it is not uncommon for a man or a woman to actually require, at some level, the feeling that their partner harbours a dark and unknown past. The particularity of this situation becomes generalised in the formal science of game theory: this set as its initial task the calculation of the concerns of the opponent in a confrontation, which would allow one to know how best to act in relation to the other party. The other's behaviour could thus be understood and reduced to a knowledge. Yet it is surely no accident that the founder of this new science, John von Neumann, could pinpoint in the development of his thinking the moments in childhood when he watched his mother gaze blankly out of a window and wondered what it was that preoccupied her. This inquiry would generate, eventually, a theory of calculation, an answer to the question of margins, of what could not be understood in the other. And, as Lacan would argue, the question of what the other wants here is quickly transformed into the question of what value we have for the other, what we must be for her. 'What do you want?' becomes translated into the question 'What am I for you?', a question which emerges with such regularity in love stories. When Hitchcock kept his silence in the presence of Doris Day on the set of *The Man Who Knew Too Much*, the being of the star was shaken, the question of her own value accentuated by the director's opacity. The fact that he hardly ever said anything made her deeply anxious as to what she meant to him, what she was. Hence one reason for the silence maintained by the analyst most of the time in psychoanalysis: the less he or she speaks, the more their opacity takes the form of the question, What do they want from me? And then, hopefully, the question of one's being, what one is for the other, can be traced in that person's history, the way they have chosen in their lives to respond to this.

There are different ways of replying to this manifestation of the desire of the other. A woman may insist on creating the same gap in the relations with those surrounding her, in stirring up desires and sustaining the desire of someone she knows for someone else. She can create a situation of unsatisfied desire, to find her own being in the gap she has authored. The question about her own identity is thus broached through the questions, 'What am I for him?' or, in a triangular relation, 'What is she for him?', both questions aiming at the problem of her own feminine identity. In such scenarios, maintaining a gap is crucial, and when the gap disappears, for whatever reason, the result is a crisis. Freud scholars have often wondered why his patient Dora slapped her grubby suitor Mr K in the famous scene by the lake. He has been pursuing Dora, while her own father conducts an affair with Mrs K. At the lake, Mr K turns to Dora and says the worst possible thing a married man can say to a woman: 'My wife means nothing to me,' a sentence which proves quite dramatic in its effects. The problem is to understand why this sentence should hurt Dora so much, since one might have assumed that this is exactly the sort of thing that she wanted him to say. We can remember the turning point for the heroine of *Rebecca* when she hears her husband's confession: not only did he not love Rebecca, he also murdered her. To de Winter's 'Rebecca meant nothing to me', the heroine responds with a new vigour, not a new breakdown. But if we read du Maurier's unpublished epilogue to *Rebecca* together with the published version, this becomes less of a contradiction. Although she is no longer the timid creature she was before meeting Mr de Winter, and although she showed her capacities after learning the truth about Rebecca's death, her life now is strangely depleted. Living in exile with her husband, her days become routine and her vivacity dimmed: and just as she had always imagined herself being seen from Rebecca's point of view, she now describes both herself and Maxim from the point of view of others, the tourists and expats who form their own images of the couple. With the subtraction of the other woman, it is as if everything that had animated her is extinguished and she is left with an emptiness that her memories can only sharpen.

To acknowledge that she is everything for the man and that the wife doesn't count may seem like exactly what Dora and the narrator of *Rebecca* want to hear, but the unhappy percussion of the scene by the lake and the fate of Mrs de Winter prove quite the contrary. Lacan's rereading of the Dora case makes the sequence clearer, as it shows the central place for Dora of the figure of Mrs K, incarnating for her the question of femininity. How is it that a woman can be loved? What interests her is what her father sees in Mrs K, and she in fact does her best to allow their relationship to continue relatively unperturbed. When Mr K tells her that his wife means nothing to him, the triangle is suddenly thrown into confusion. Dora has recreated with Mr K the same relation that her father has with Mrs K: a woman is desired by a man, although they do not have sex. Her father loves Mrs K beyond Dora, just as Mr K loves Dora beyond his wife. If his wife in fact means nothing to him, then she is no longer situated in a triangle, and, furthermore, due to the homology of the two sets of relations, she no longer counts for her father, since her place is structurally identical with the place of Mrs K in the first triangle. By knocking out Mrs K, the man has both subtracted the central feminine player and knocked Dora out of a carefully constructed scheme. There is no longer a gap between the two of them, and the triangles collapse.

A man might have a very different response to the preservation of this gap, a response which in fact endeavours to abolish it, to do away with the question of the desire of the other. In its place are put verbal activities and rituals such as counting, reducing the horizon of the world to the blotting paper of language. And even ubiquity. The man who is always there, whether you need him or not, will do his best to be present as a response to exactly the same problem, the warding off of the dangerous emergence of the desire of his partner. If he is always there, absence is banished and he can make of himself literally the appendage to the woman. The world is complete, with the unfortunate consequence that the world is a dead one, as continued presence and suffocation are one and the same thing. This is no doubt the reason why many men are convinced of the existence of extra-terrestrial life forms. It is often argued, with some spite, that women, naturally superstitious, are eager to embrace the ETs in their love of the beyond, but it is a fact that many men are equally or even more enthusiastic for aliens. But their affirmatively answered question, 'Is there life up there?', is simply a cover for another question, 'Is there life down here?', this time negatively answered, with a denial of the living dimension, the desiring dimension of their spouses. The young lady who put a stool in the path of the Milesian philosopher Thales understood this exactly. His study of the heavens directed his gaze upward, and he thus failed to see what lay on earth, tumbling over the stool and realising, perhaps, that it would not do to ignore terrestrial attractions. This explains the amazing popularity of the television series *The X Files*: the agreeable team of agents Mulder and Scully spend all their time following up their suspicions that anything strange that happens down here must be the work of powers up there. But the most fascinating thing that happens down here is in fact something that doesn't happen: Mulder and Scully sleeping together. If they did, the stars would be depopulated considerably. Back on earth, it's best for people to forget that they are living with an alien, and to confine the latter's intrusion to the habitual abduction. This occurrence, affecting a large percentage of the American population, may not be as simple as it appears. What the research would have to uncover is whether the percentage that claims to have been abducted is the same as the percentage that claims to believe in ET: if not, then abduction becomes another item to be added to a list of excuses which includes working late at the office.

The gap that human beings dread so much may be linked to the emergence of an alien desire, even if this is completely absent from consciousness. When it emerges, we lose the mastery of ourselves and become split apart and divided: or, as Lacan put it, we fade. There must be a good reason, after all, why so many people avoid stepping on the cracks between paving stones. When psychoanalysts first turned their attention to this problem, they found that the everyday aversion formed part of a superstition: if you stepped on the crack, something bad would happen to either yourself or a loved one. From this, it was easy to infer the presence of an unconscious desire to actually do harm to that person, and hence the symptom could be seen as an attempt to ward off the evil thought. On a more general level, it shows that the habitat of troubling and disturbing desire is in the place of gaps: so, to avoid the desire, the effort to abolish the gap. When a gap proves necessary, it gets treated with words, which is why doors have got little mottoes and messages written above them. A door is a gap, a space in between inside and outside, and so the tendency to inscribe either a good luck charm or some legend to deter evil spirits. What's being deterred is the presence of a desire, whose only home is the space in between two things.

The paradox for the man who tries to avoid this dimension by thinking and counting is that although language can be used to construct a fortress to ward off the living, desiring dimension of human beings, it is also what makes that dimension come back. Freud's patient the Rat Man constructed endless series of prayers and supplications to ward off his unpleasant wishes, but as he prayed and endeavoured to banish the sexual dimension with words, it came back to divide him, in the insults and negations that were to haunt the cracks in his speech. If he said, 'May God protect him', an unknown power would insert a 'not' and when he devised a protective formula, *Glejisamen*, to block out unseemly thoughts linked to his cousin when he masturbated, the word *saman* (semen) would return to contaminate it. At one moment, he even developed the embarrassing symptom of asking his interlocutors to repeat their sentences until he was absolutely sure that he had understood exactly what it was they were saying. In the postmodern world, where we are forever being reminded that speech always has several different meanings, this is a very unhelpful symptom to live with. What would have happened if he had attended a congress of post-structuralists and insisted that everything said be reduced to a univocal meaning? If everything can be reduced to thinking, desire is blotted out and its denial seems to save the thinker from anxiety, but, as these examples show, this is no simple business.

When Bishop Berkeley summoned his doctor, the latter reported that the Idealist had the idea he was ill, and it took much effort to make him accept the idea of health. For this misunderstood man, the world was a world of ideas, and yet their perpetual activity could not abolish the gap between them. According to a popular impression of the Bishop's doctrine, not only were ideas everywhere, but each idea had to have a subject, someone to be having them. This introduces a number of questions of an apparently abstract nature, such as 'Do the stars exist when we're not looking at them?' This question is in fact posed in a particular form by many children: will the furniture, they wonder, behave any differently at night when they are no longer there to survey it? Will the toys come to life and engage in an intrigue?

At the horizon of these inquiries is the real question of what happens in one part of the house when they are not looking: for example, the parents' bedroom. This is the area of interest which is shifted with more charm to the contents of the house. Or, of course, from their own body: will the furniture display as much wilfulness as their own genitals, coming to life regardless of their instructions? The psychoanalyst Mary Chadwick described the case of a young girl who had often heard her mother use the expression 'before you were born or thought of', and hence concluded that her birth was the result of the united thoughts of her parents. She then developed the Berkeleyan notion that she would only continue to exist for as long as her parents thought of her, an idea which not only shows the affinity of a child-

hood preoccupation and a philosophical theory but als
provides a clue as to the strange relation many people hav
to posterity. It is not unheard of for someone to explai
their desire for children in terms of the wish to be remem
bered: once they cease to exist, they can endure as a mem
ory in the minds of their descendants. This bizarre idea i
thus connected to the avoidance of fading, the determina
tion to keep on persisting as an idea and to do away wit
the presence of gaps. It is thus not surprising that it is me
who insist on having the most elaborate tombs and memori
als. If it is so important to make everything an idea, t
absorb everything into language, even the discontinuity o
their own death has to be treated in the same way. As fo
Berkeley, the circumstances of his own passing away pro
vide one answer to the Idealist question: he expired, i
seems, in his chair at tea without the least noise or even th
notice of the company that was present. The idea of th
Bishop was thus not dependent on the ideas of those aroun
him, and he could, as he passed away, become a true ide
perhaps for the first time.

We do not know if Berkeley was especially worried abou
stepping on the cracks between paving stones, but he wa
certainly quite anxious about the possibility of fading. Thi
took the form of his fascination with the religious debate o
'ceasing to be'. What happened between death and th
moment of resurrection? If one rejected the more Catholi
notions of a sort of intermediary waiting area, this was
difficult question to answer. Did the soul, for example, con
tinue to think or did it just sleep, and if so, did sleepin
count in any way as a form of thinking? Berkeley's studen
notebooks are filled with meditations on this theme of th
possibilities of 'ceasing to be'; the crucial question wa
whether there was a little gap between death and the resur
rection, just as there is a gap between the moment of fallin

asleep and the moment of waking. According to one view, the soul indeed expires at death, but only temporarily, until the Deity restores life to it with the body. Alternatively, it remains unconscious after death until the Last Day. The details of such polemics are involved and complex, but one could argue that the real stake of the debate revolved around the idea of the fading of the subject, the point of failing consciousness, the gap which emerged in the series of religious times after death. We can see such a fading quite literally in the life of the Bishop, when, attending an execution as a student, he became curious as to what ideas a man hanging might have. With his friend Contarine, he arranges to be hung until a signal for release at the right time, a signal which the future Bishop failed to give, falling fainting to the ground. The thirst for ideas, to absorb even the limit experience of the dying into the field of thinking, produced less an idea here than the fading of the subject. John Cleese favoured the same principle in *Fawlty Towers* when, on failing to recall the name of a guest, he pantomimed a fainting spell instead. In the place where the word was lacking, the subject faded, and hence the reason why, for the obsessional man, it is of no small importance to remember not only numbers but names.

If the Bishop was so keen to make everything an idea, we could ask the further question of whether he ever forgot to buy groceries. Where so many men do their best to avoid gaps, they often tend to create them in a humble household way. Although they may insist on having a double supply of everything, one item gets left out. This contrasts with overshopping, in which a purchase is doubled, buying two of the same thing in case the first becomes worn out or stolen. They thus purchase too much, be it a costly article or a trivial household product. Now, the problem is the following: if these overshoppers buy a double supply of many products, there is always at least one thing which they 'forget': there will be something which is only bought at the last minute or once the supply has already been exhausted. Some people buy a ten-pack carton of cigarettes to ensure that they are never without, whilst others, even if they can afford to make such a purchase, always wait until they have run out of cigarettes before buying the next pack. For the one there is too much, for the other too little. Bergler called this pattern the 'mechanism of small deprivations': in both instances, the latent idea is of being left wanting. The question we need to ask is why it is that someone who is so careful to avoid gaps, to stop any idea of a lack emerging, should ensure that in certain circumstances, something is indeed left out. One might reply that it is less a question of aiming consciously to be deprived, simply that since thinking can't get rid of gaps, they will always return in one form or other.

This mechanism does not only confine itself to trivial objects: it may, for both men and women, concern the living partner. Some men are compelled to have a woman 'in reserve' even if they profess to be reasonably satisfied with an ongoing relationship. They don't necessarily sleep with this third party, but she must 'be there', available and waiting. Some women, likewise, may 'collect' men and only end a relationship with a man once someone else has been secured: there is thus always an overlap, a surplus supply of man. Although these situations have an apparent symmetry, the structure is not exactly identical. A woman may keep a man in reserve so that when she switches, she will still have a place as the object of a man's desire: she will be able to continue to perpetuate the question, 'What am I for him?' or, if she happens to be interested in the penis, it will still be there despite the changing identity of the partner. It is less the personality of the man that counts here than the fact that there is someone there to incarnate a desire (and/or an organ), which gives the formula to describe bachelors: can't live with them, can't live without them. For a man, however, the woman in reserve may take on a value as the one who is kept out of the romantic game: he may not sleep with her, but he goes crazy if someone else does. She thus has the role of a woman who is available, who is not connected to a man and with whom he doesn't sleep. The obvious interpretation of this phenomenon would be to link the list of qualities with the mother: contrary to the real oedipal situation in which the father is present, she is now available, separated and, respectfully, untouched. But rather than seeing this simply as a set of claims on the parent, the woman who is kept in reserve could be identified with the phallus itself: kept out of the game of lovers and out of harm's way, it incarnates the lost element that must be preserved at all costs. Only once it is hidden away like this can the man assume some pretence of virility with another woman. What he's got to lose is kept neatly out of harm's way.

Having a woman in reserve is not, however, the prerogative of men, and we find a female version in the famous Amiens episode of Vita Sackville-West. When Vita and Violet Trefusis had their tempestuous row at Amiens in 1920, it revolved around exactly this question of the separation of a woman from contact with the penis. The two women escaped their husbands on a mad trip to France shortly after Violet's wedding to Denys Trefusis. He left them at Amiens, returning to London, only to come back with Vita's husband on a rescue mission, piloting a plane with single-handed valour to get there in time. After this brave adventure, the anxious men were only to find two women who laughed at them when they showed up at the hotel. Until Vita's husband Harold played his trump: are you sure, he asked his wife, that Violet has been faithful to you? The two women had made a pact before Violet's marriage that no coitus was to take place: Denys' penis was strictly out of bounds, but now Harold suggested that things might have been otherwise. Vita's fury knew no limits here. Although Violet had done everything she could to make Vita react in the preceding months, even marrying Denys in order to get Vita to press her claim on her, this new development was hardly expected. Rushing downstairs, she demanded of Denys whether he had ever been 'really married' to Violet. 'If you tell me you have,' she continued, 'I swear to you I will never set eyes on Violet again.' And yet, despite all of this, Vita says that she knew Violet was a virgin: it was thus less coitus that was at stake than contact with the penis. What Vita wanted instead was absolute devotion: as she would say, what mattered to her was whether Violet belonged to her or not, even if she herself was never willing to belong completely to the other woman. There is thus a separation between the real penis and the symbolic principle of sacrifice which Vita had to sustain at all costs. The organ lost out when compared with the principle, the sign of loss, of what has been given up. The moment it seemed that Violet had been unfaithful to this principle and that the rule of sacrifice had not been followed, all hell would break loose.

Poor Harold and Denys. Despite the boldness of their plane trip, they appear mortified when compared with the vivacity of their wives. But rather than assuming that such a dulling of spirit is simply a quality of the male sex, one may try to account for its genesis, in just the same way that the extreme obedience of a small child cannot be explained away as a natural attribute: rather, one has to ask the question of what makes such an obedience possible at all. When men seem a bit lifeless and petty, overly tidy and fastidious in the making of lists, popular opinion calls them anal. The classical psychoanalytic view is that such features are a consequence of repressed hostility, linked to the anal phase of childhood in which excrements are expelled with a view to harming the caregiver. Ernest Jones devoted many papers to these themes, and came to the conclusion that hatred and the history of one's sphincters could not be separated. In the process of sphincter education, he thinks, the loved parent obstructs the pleasure of the child, generating a hostility which has more ravaging effects for the man. This is due to the fact that, for Jones, hostility to the mother is a more natural part of the female's 'normal development'. Since it isn't for the male, it will be more difficult for him to deal with the ambivalence of his feelings and they may continue to torture him throughout the course of his life. But can anatomy explain everything here? On the contrary, it would seem as if what matters is not simply the body and its mechanisms, but rather the way in which these are caught up in the relations with the parents, relations which involve ideas, meanings and desires.

As a child grows up, it is the parents who speak to him or her about the body and stipulate the rules which they have fixed for the control of its organs. Expelling and withholding faeces will therefore be given a specific meaning in the relation to the adult: for example, as something good or bad, desired or condemned. In a position of helplessness and dependency, it is a privileged moment when the child is required by the parent to manifest its own subjectivity: as the caregiver asks the child to comply, the latter receives, as it were, a first form of power, of the possibility of refusing, of asserting a will individualised from that of the parents. And in a general sense, the birth of subjectivity is *always linked to refusals*: that's all a child has got. Anatole France said quite seriously that he formed his opinions on any given subject by taking the view that was diametrically opposed to that of his parents. Even when the view is the same, it is different since it is his own. When an adult asks a child to stop doing something, the child may perform the prohibited action just once more, as if the stopping was introduced by himself rather than by the adult. As the great observer of child development René Spitz phrased the latent idea: 'I am doing this because I want to and I am not doing what you want. I have a will of my own and even when it is the same as yours, it is different because it is my own.' And hence the phase of anal stubbornness noted by all psychoanalytic observers of children.

The key here to understand the link between the bodily mechanism and the relation with the parent is the idea of demand. The manifestation of subjectivity will emerge as an opposition or a deferred compliance to what the child is being asked to do. And in this context, the demand of the parent can take on a very special value: it can become, as Lacan argued, the very thing that the child searches for and without which he is left completely lost. Which means that someone's whole existence is left suspended on the demands coming from others. So involved is the subject with the demand of the other, that it comes to function as the object of desire: what he wants, therefore, is to be demanded to do something. In Reik's formulation, if such men are ready to do what they are asked, they do not know what to do when they are not asked. They can only function if there is some form of demand which requires them to do something, and furthermore, in contrast to the hysteric, it is this which gives them much satisfaction. If you ask a hysteric to do something, the immediate response may be to refuse, whereas the obsessional will show, on the contrary, how good he is. But the establishment of the anal structure involves more than this: if the demands of the educators are so privileged, what happens to the noxious object itself around which these demands once circled?

This object is supposed to be a bad one, rejected by the parents as unseemly, and yet it is the result of a valued activity, the motion which results from the infant's good-will. The infant might have been a 'good' little boy or girl, but the object he or she has produced is removed with distaste. This duplicity which surrounds excrement has its place in sexual life. When the young Marcel Pagnol finds the first girl he can idealise, his romance continues unchecked until the moment he hears a toilet flush and realises that this beautiful and dazzling creature has bowels like himself. His love is completely destroyed and the reveries which had caused so much amusement in the Pagnol household are suddenly banished. As the toilet flush echoes in his head, the web of romance he has constructed around her and her family dissolves and the poet father becomes merely a sad absinthe drinker, the perfect mother an affected and troubled dissembler. Freud tells us also of how his patient the Wolf Man was tormented by doubts about whether Christ had a bottom or not, and his anal preoccupations would contaminate the things he held most sacred. Such doubts, which are articulated quite often by children and continue to haunt the thought of not a few adults, were once questions seriously debated by the theologians. Were there excrements in paradise and did the son of God excrete like the rest of us? And, crucially, as Thomas Aquinas wondered, at the moment of resurrection, would the pious rise with their bowels? Which demonstrates the centrality of the question of whether excrement is or isn't a part of the body.

In this anal structure, there is thus a tension between the linguistic side of the exchange, which involves the articulated demands of the educators, and the 'object' side, the element which is literally thrown away and rejected. This becomes crucial when we realise that at a certain level language itself does not recognise us, it is not built for the specificity and individuality of human beings, but is imposed on us. To the extent that we are real individuals, we are not just identical to the words, ideals and dreams of those around us. We are, in a sense, rejected or excluded from this field, and so an equivalence may be established between the subject and their excrement: at one level, a child may think, they literally are their excrement, as a left-over, rejected remainder. And this is where an unconscious enjoyment becomes lodged. One might evoke here the observation made by child psychologists that when a mother fails to respond in the expected way, when an opaque blankness becomes substituted for a friendly smile, a child will reply with a reference to its own body. When the mother becomes strange, the child may touch itself, sucking its thumb or trying in some way to stimulate the body surface. In other words, where there is a failure to recognise, an element of the body takes on a special value.

This may be seen clearly at those moments when someone has to take on a place in the linguistic world, a new appointment, an important social engagement, or even simply a trip to a public place. In this privileged space, the subject becomes what schoolboys call the misfit: a stain. At such moments the obsessional will describe how he feels like someone who shouldn't be there, who doesn't have a place, who feels like the excrement that is in the wrong place at the wrong time. And it is no accident that we use expressions like 'Shit!' when something unwanted or unexpected happens, something that doesn't have a place there. The structure here is a constant: these feelings of being out of place, which go to the very heart of the obsessional, will become accentuated at those moments when he is somewhere which serves to embody the world of language, the social network, the space which, not being built for him, can never fully recognise him. As Reik once pointed out, we are not just born *inter faeces et urinas*, we live there.

This dimension of the stain returned with regularity for the Puritan general Cromwell in the famous daubing incidents. At an important social function, he 'excremented' himself, daubing his own clothes in muck and then dancing with others in order to soil them. Later, at his daughter's wedding, a moment at which, as he knew, his symbolic role as father was appealed to, he started to throw sack-posset among the ladies to soil their fine clothes and began to daub their chairs with wet sweetmeats as they were sitting down. This materialising of the stain would emerge again at the crucial moment of signing the death warrant of the King, as he daubs Marten's face with ink, in each instance compelled to make something there which shouldn't be there. The excrement reappears when it is a question of assuming a symbolic place in the world, as if the stain, and not words, would incarnate what he was in relation to everything outside, his own little individual signature coming into the place where the world didn't give him one. It is a position in relation not just to the social circuit but, in a more general sense, to language as such. Where words are embodied, so will an element that shouldn't be there. This explains a further question: why is mucus so regularly found on library books? A form of excrement, it marks the presence of the subject in a world of words, their being as a stain, showing within the space of a printed page that subjectivity is never entirely reducible to language. And that's why if excrement is found near words, words are found near excrement: how else could one explain the odd human propensity to graffiti toilets?

Or indeed the fact that many people can only go to the toilet if they are reading something. If Cromwell's daubings involve literally a waste product, another example illustrates how it may be speech itself which is used to create a stain in language. When people go to the theatre, they rarely think about what's happening on the stage. Whether they like it or not, as Lacan observed, their thoughts turn to the events of the day, to their various problems, to their duties of the future. And it is a fact that with great frequency, men have the transitory thought of making a great eruption, jumping onto the stage, exclaiming something in a moment of silence, crying out in an action that would turn the attentions of all spectators to them. Now, this may be understood along the lines we have discussed, as a way of avoiding a gap. If a pause in dialogue incarnates a gap in language for the man, he may have the idea to fill it with more words, but it is the eruptive, exclamatory character of the interruption which is the clue here.

Reik discusses a patient who had the intense impulse during the most solemn scene of *Parsifal* at the Vienna State Opera to shout at the top of his voice 'Matzoth-balls!' The impulse became so powerful that only his flight from the auditorium saved him from the scandal that would no doubt have resulted if his projected action had been realised. Why, Reik asks, was the impulse so strong and what were its origins? As he suggests, there is the address to his family who were present at the opera that night, a family who had converted in order to lose their Jewish origins. The Matzoth-balls, from this perspective, are the sign of the family truth that cannot be silenced, the parental infidelity to their religious faith. But there is also the Cromwellian dimension, the fact that in imagining this scene, he is being somewhere he shouldn't be, becoming a presence, through his voice, which embodies that which should be hidden and which, when it appears, has exactly this function of the stain.

This would explain the well-known phenomenon of the transformation of the meek. There are people who always do what they're told, and enjoy that. The demand of others has no doubt been privileged, but sometimes they explode in the strangest ways, indicating that something more complicated than the simple mechanistic idea of a build up of anger and its release is at stake. As Edmund Gosse is instructed by his father in the writings of the Old Testament, he suddenly erupts, 'Oh, how I do hate the law.' The manifestation of subjectivity, the stain and the explosive quality are all combined in the simple ejaculation. This shows how the anal structure operates, and nuances those psychoanalytic explanations which understand volatility simply in terms of supposed repressed hostility. The clinical proof of this is in the fact that, as Freud's students noted, interpreting latent hostility to an obsessional – although this is what many analysts spend a long time doing – has few clinical effects. Which isn't to deny that there may be lots of hostility, just that, to effect this, you have to look somewhere else.

It has often been argued that it is this latent hostility which makes getting over the loss of a loved one so difficult. What is more difficult to bear than the sudden emergence of a negative thought about someone loved and lost? The problem, Freud thought, is that when hostile currents are focused on the departed one, the process of mourning becomes increasingly difficult. At a conscious level, when such negative thoughts appear, they are often followed by a supplication, a visit to the grave or, if the person is still living, some friendly action. The treatment of this kind of hostility is no doubt crucial to the work of mourning, but it is often examined to the neglect of the other aspect of this process, the selection of details. We have seen the importance of details for the beginning and end of love relations, an importance which is in no way diminished when it comes to getting through the grief of a disappointed love. When a loved one is mourned, lost through death, departure or desertion, to go through the process of mourning is to pass through a certain collection of details. The question here is to ask why it is that to work through a broken love affair will be to focus not on a person as such but on a small set of traits, as if the process of mourning is itself a process of selection. Stendhal tells the story of a beau who returns from a long journey to join his loved one. He finds her in the grounds of her country house, and, as she gives him her hand, he feels a sense of certainty that she loves him. As they stroll along the garden paths, her dress catches on an acacia bush. After learning of her subsequent infidelity to him, he insists that her greeting was the sure sign of her love even if he can remember no detail of that meeting, a sign, for Stendhal, that love it was not. And yet despite this apparent absence of details, the man remains visibly shaken by the sight of an acacia, and this, Stendhal says, is the only distinct memory he preserved of the happiest moment of his life.

Recovering from the abyss of a broken love, a young woman finds herself humming a tune from Mozart, a composer she has no special knowledge of or liking for. The melody pursues her, at work, in the subway, as she walks to her home. Suddenly, some days later, she remembers that this was the music which the man who left her had once said should be played at his funeral. From this moment onwards, the work of mourning moves on, and her torment begins to lessen. The question here is why it was necessar for her to remember: she could have either remembered at the start or not at all. Why did it take a couple of days for the connection to be made? The actress Billie Whitelaw writes about a similar experience. Whenever she would hear the popular tune 'You Are My Sunshine', she would be gripped by a sadness which she could not understand. Thirty years later, her mother tells her that after her father's death she would cry listening to this song, as it reminded her of his going away. After hearing this from her mother, her own sadness vanishes. Again, a connection is made and a painful feeling is lifted, indicating that the work of mourning is linked to the process of establishing connections, junctions between feelings and ideas which direct the sadness to particular details.

This takes a long time, and no doubt explains why Proust wrote such long books: as he tried to pinpoint each of the qualities which marked the loves of his youth, volume became added to volume in the effort not to omit any detail. Even after he had written the words 'La Fin' to his life's work, he could not stop himself from returning to correct and refine his descriptions, showing the impossibility for him of putting the full stop to signal that the selection of details was complete. The past here fades only once it has become the present. Misunderstanding such connections between a feeling and an idea is as commonplace as it is confusing. When Rebecca West complained of her uneasiness on seeing jagged mountain ranges, it might well have been inferred that she was afraid of heights, or that she had suffered a trauma once amidst the peaks or that the uneven nature of the mountains represented the uneven internal state of her emotional life. This sort of interpretation is what many people receive who are in some kind of psychological treatment, yet the conclusions would be less absurd if they were grounded in real associative connections. As for Rebecca, her uneasiness left her when she realised that the jagged peaks reminded her of the graphs of the rise and fall of copper prices that she had often watched her father anxiously scrutinise as a child.

The pain of something lost is often explained as evoking a gap in the psyche itself, a point where words are lacking, and the only way it can be dealt with is by focusing on the details which mark its edges, its contours. This process has been equated with what is known in psychoanalysis as 'working through', but it is a key question to see whether mourning and working through are one and the same thing. The problem is that mourning can take place outside a psychoanalysis, but, as Freud argued, working through is something peculiar to the analytic process. So if details are crucial for both, what are the differences? It is an amazing fact of psychoanalytic history that the very process which Freud saw as distinguishing analysis from other forms of therapy has hardly ever received any real attention. When Freud first introduced the term translated as 'working through' (*Durcharbeitung*) in his article 'Remembering, Repeating and Working Through', it evoked a reference to musical theory, the 'working out' which takes place between the introduction and the conclusion of a sonata. This was not lost to Freud's early students, and the decision to translate the term as working 'through' and not 'out' may be because working out is what you do in a gym, not in a consulting room. In musical theory, working out, or development, is the time which involves the treatment of the theme introduced at the start of the piece. It is now complicated and elaborated by a varied treatment in different keys: the theme is disintegrated into its constituent parts and these are then combined and varied before returning, in the final cadence, to the original key of the introduction. There is thus a tension between the working through and repetition, a tension that musicologists have sometimes situated as the key dynamic of the sonata form and which we find in the title of Freud's paper. The implication is that the element that is repeated, be it a musical sequence or a pattern in one's own life, must be broken down into its parts and new links established between these parts.

If we take the musical reference seriously, the question of what an analytic working through is about becomes clearer. The obvious answer is a simple one: a working through is just the time between an interpretation and the disappearance of a symptom. But this is disproved by the clinical fact that many people miraculously lose their symptoms after one or two visits to the analyst's office! And this for the excellent reason that losing a few symptoms is a small price to pay for safeguarding one's neurosis: a psychoanalysis can thus be avoided. Freud called this the 'flight into health'. Even if, during one of these visits, the patient is told some interpretation, the effect is less a working through than a sort of shock therapy. Bergler was fond of the following comparison: a man has been stealing from the cash register of the store where he works. One morning, after a drunken night out with his friends, his boss remarks that he looks unusually pale. This is immediately understood as the sign that the boss is aware of his thefts: and so, for a while, he stops stealing. Although the intervention was effective for a time, it had nothing to do with either the awareness of the theft or its causes.

The disappearance of symptoms in itself is thus not an adequate criterion to determine the presence of working through, and in fact what the musical analogy suggests is that it is less the disappearance of symptoms than their re-emergence which testifies to the analytic process having operated. After all, the last moment of the second musical time will end with the re-evocation of the initial key of the movement, in order to introduce the conclusion. What was there at the start comes back, and, curious as it may seem, this can be observed clinically. Many analytic scholars tried to explain why it was that after long years of arduous analytic work and the disappearance of the most serious symptoms, these would often reappear in the last stages of an analysis. The most interesting and the oddest explanation of this phenomenon was put forward in the 1960s by Rudolf Ekstein. He had the idea that symptoms are like actors in the theatre and that after the long spectacle which is an analysis, they come back on stage at the end to bid the audience farewell. This idea is so curious that one is tempted to try to save it, but if we apply the musical analogy, the implication is that things might come back but they won't be quite the same. In a fine piece of music, as the initial motif is broken down, recombined and rearranged, its meaning and its effects on the listener change. When it returns at the end, its resonances may be profoundly different from what they were at the start. Something has happened between the end and the beginning, which makes the same element a stranger to itself. Which is one of the things that psychoanalysis is all about. The idea one entertains consciously at the start will be adjusted and corrected through the symbolic work of the analytic process, to produce something new, a sequence which may be found in many other fields of research. When mathematicians took the intuitive idea of a polyhedron and tried to formalise its properties rigorously, what happened was not a making concrete of the original basic image of a solid with plane faces and straight edges, but rather a strange new definition in terms of stretchability and projectibility. Likewise, as the science of crystals developed, the basic image of the crystal as a hard, glassy object became altered to such an extent that many things that had once been classified as crystal ceased to be so, and other things such as certain liquids became included. This is exactly what a working through is about: a basic conception is subjected to a logical treatment, generating contradictions and inconsistencies, until a new perspective emerges as a result of the symbolic work. It is perhaps this confrontation with contradictions and inconsistencies which is one of the factors separating a mourning from a real working through.

This is by no means the same thing as having a knowledge about oneself. It happens from time to time that a patient sketches a brilliant picture of their own neurosis right at the start of a treatment, and yet, as is well known, this knowledge has no effect whatsoever. Many years later they may come back to the same point, and even utter the very same words about themselves, yet these words will now have a completely different meaning. What has happened in between is illustrated by a problem of the philosophers. A viewer and his neighbour are both watching a tennis match on television which is relayed live from the courts. But unbeknown to the second viewer, an alien spaceship has alighted on the roof of his building and a devious simulation of the match is replacing the authentic transmission. At the courts, player C wins, and in the simulation, player C wins as well. The question asked by philosophers is the following, Does the second viewer know that player C has won, or does he just believe it? What this fanciful example shows is that if knowledge is going to count at all, it must be had in the right way: in this example, through the correct causal channels which lead from the courts to the camera to the TV set. It is thus a question of *how* knowledge is arrived at rather than *what* knowledge consists of. And in the analytic context, although knowledge is by no means the goal as such of an analysis, it shows that the route matters just as much as the destination, since it may turn out that one was at the place of the destination all along, yet without knowing it. Knowledge, to matter at all, must be purchased at no small price. The beginning may be formally the same as the end, but there is a difference nonetheless, as the organisation of music shows.

The problem, particularly in the treatment of obsessionals, is that there is a basic block to examining and unravelling the channels which, in the philosophers' example, lead from the courts to the viewer at home. The ample speech of these people aims, at one level, at providing all the necessary information to the analyst, but in a way designed to block access to other vital elements. The analyst is only supposed to interpret the material he receives, and so, through the calculated pacing and withholding of associations, the obsessional may try to guide the analyst through a part of his labyrinth according to his own rules. Thus, to interpret, the analyst may signal a link between associations that the patient has not thought of himself and which involves material from a distant session. Which produces a very singular effect. If people get angry from time to time when things don't work out, what we see in these precise analytic contexts is not anger but indignation. It's the idea, 'You may be right, but you do not have the right to be right since you don't have the right to know that.' The analyst does not have the right because he has not been guided to his conclusion by the plotted architecture of the patient's speech.

The same situation is well known in courts of law. Someone is accused of a misdemeanour, and although clearly guilty, defends himself with great zeal, to the point that he may genuinely believe he is innocent. The point is that he *is* innocent from the perspective of the information delivered: he has only said so much, there is only so much evidence, so, although objectively guilty, the other has no right to accuse him. The other does not have the right to know that he is guilty. The fault of the subject is shifted to the other, as it is the other who trespasses here in judging independently. This is the structure that separates anger from indignation, which always concerns a relation to knowledge.

The symmetry of beginnings and endings is thus complicated. The same element may be present at start and finish, yet one's relation to it has changed. When Theseus entered the maze built by Daedalus, he exited from the same point, yet his life, and the meaning of entry and exit, had changed for him. A labyrinth may forever remain a labyrinth, but whether one is inside it or surveying it from above will alter completely the state of one's confusion: its ability to perplex depends on this perspective point. The motif of a labyrinth of love was popular in medieval times, and in the classical maze, unlike many of the more modern versions, there is only one gate: entry and exit are one and the same. There is also never any choice: the person who enters the maze follows one single path and there are no internal choices to be made as to which way to go. The real decision here is therefore whether to enter the maze or not, rather than which route to take once inside. And as for the centre, the classical maze will make sure that the path to it is the longest possible. If there is a link to love in this detail, it is in the fact that the function of the classical labyrinth is to delay an arrival. The encounter with whatever lies at the centre is thus deferred, just as love at a distance is always careful to avoid a confrontation with its object.

When Dudley Moore spent so much time in *10* chasing the woman he had fallen for, the excitement is in the delay, not in the eventual encounter: when he finally goes to bed with Bo Derek, it turns out to be the last thing he wants, showing how desire and its object are two different things. It is an interesting feature of this film that it is always assumed that *10* refers to Dudley Moore's grading of the woman he's tailing, but this is never once mentioned: she is counted, in fact, as an '11'. The only time that the figure '10' actually gets used is when Moore's estranged partner Julie Andrews takes a break from her stage rehearsal: a '10' refers here to a pause (like 'Take 5'), a delay rather than an appreciation, and thus the '10' of the title finds its place. Not as the numerical value of the woman, but as the description of the delayer, the maze wanderer whose desire is sustained as unfulfilled for most of the film. Hence the reasonable project of making a sequel.

If the process of moving around a maze is thus different from reaching its centre, there is still the question of what fate awaits the wanderer when he eventually gets there. For Dudley Moore, it was to realise the vanity of his illusions, and that the sustained idealisation of the woman would crumble when he confronted the doped up oddity that awaited him in bed. While he could watch the sexual activities of his virile neighbours with great excitement through a telescope, when he is deprived of this phantasy frame, his desire collapses as he is now inside the picture rather than being the one who is watching, and waiting, from the outside. Indeed, such reversals are the rule when the process of desiring, the hunt for the object, seems to reach its goal. When Daphne du Maurier was being chased by her wealthy host Otto Khan at the edge of a Norwegian fjord, she turned his aspirations into chaos when she gave him what he wanted: stripping naked there and then, she plunged into the water, and the embarrassed magnate was left to find another object for his pursuits. The ancient example of

Hypatia is even more precise in its unveiling of what lies at the root of desire: as a student speaks of his love for her with all the rhetoric of Platonic philosophy, she shows him a used menstrual towel. 'You are in love with this, young man,' she says, 'not with the Beautiful,' the horrific object and not the Platonic Idea, which the process of loving is aimed at obscuring. Perhaps it was this vignette that inspired the medieval doctor Bernard of Gordon to prescribe as a cure for the sickness of love a detailed confrontation with the sexual organs of an old woman and rags stained with menstrual blood. After this, how could the besotted lover continue to construct his vain artifice? If such objects are what lie at the heart of the maze, it demonstrates that what one searches for the most is not necessarily something linked to one's own good.

And in the classical maze, what lies at the centre is something very different from love: it is not love but death, embodied in the horror of the Minotaur. Lacan compared obsessional neurosis to a labyrinth, suggesting that the centre of the maze, the point to be avoided at all costs and yet around which life is organised, is death. Freud and his students interpreted this aspect of obsession as the result of death wishes directed to those one loved: to defend against these, the subject would construct a whole system of rituals at the cost of his own mortification. A different sort of death would thus, ironically, be introduced. As the rituals are multiplied and become ever more oppressive, the result is a loss of vitality, a life regulated and burdened with endless obsessive rituals, to give many men an existence which is less a life than a timetable. It can also, on occasion, generate the illusion of an exuberance which seems quite the opposite yet is equally mortifying. Reik describes the case of a man who is tortured with anxiety about doing some harm to his young son. This had begun to invade his life from the moment he had started to doubt whether he had not once banged the boy on the head with a door knob as he entered a room. He was then forced to take precautions to assure himself that no harm would be done. But, he pondered, what would his friends and colleagues think if they saw him in the middle of a sentence stick out his arm to measure the distance to the door? And yet by this improvised measurement he wished to free himself from the torturing doubt. The solution came by becoming a changed man: as he spoke he now threw out his arms in expansive gestures. He would make an animated gesture when he spoke of something over there, or when he pointed out how large some object was, or, on meeting a friend, by spreading his arms and burlesquing an extravagance of feeling. Yet the new radiance noted by his companions was simply the tortured disguise of ill wishes. The blossoming of his character was thus subject to the same rules which cancel vitality, engaging to others perhaps but fierce and uncompromising in its requirements for himself.

Now, the passage through the labyrinth has not a little in common with the idea of working through: connections are established, the familiar becomes the unfamiliar and, by modifying the framework of one's perspective, one's confusion may become clarified. But whereas the analogy of the maze indicates the importance of a change of perspective, Lacan's remarks suggest that it is not just a question of oneself looking at things in a new way. This, after all, is the principle of self-help books: remember a few maxims and things will change, you will be able to see things from a new perspective at last. What needs to be distinguished is the fact that the point from which the maze suddenly becomes clear is a strange one: the perspective point which allows one to see is one's own, but also someone else's. This is a startling proposition, that your life is organised from someone else's perspective, and you do not even realise that consciously. In his Tenth Letter, Seneca urges the virtue of self-reliance, but then, to the mystification of some of his readers, he continues in the Eleventh Letter to advise thinking of someone else, some prized being, watching that person's every act. This is no doubt the reason why many people have problems running their own business. Economic difficulties aside, it poses the question of what it means to 'work for oneself': strictly speaking, this is impossible, and without the figure of the employer, it becomes necessary to produce new forms of this prized being to whom are offered up the fruits of one's labour. Self-reliance and reliance on this other might seem a recipe for discord, but there is no real contradiction here. From the psychoanalytic viewpoint, the confusions of the maze will reveal their logic once this special perspective point has been pinpointed and revealed as what it was all along: someone else's view, which has been made into one's own.

Once again, we can turn to Daphne du Maurier for an example. *Rebecca* tells the story of one woman's going into the place of another woman, moving into the house and even the dress of the dead wife. If this is a story which may be lived, in one way or another, by each woman, there can be no original author, and it is no surprise to learn that after the publication of her book in 1938, a priority dispute took place, in which both the Brazilian author Nabuco and those representing the American writer Edwina MacDonald claimed that the story was their own. This dispute between women is another version of the narrative contained in *Rebecca*, the story of one woman claiming another's place, and if the structure is so general that no final author can be claimed, it is very different from the traditional priority disputes over who came first: when Newton and Leibniz battled over the invention of the calculus, it was less a question of their sexed identity than of genealogies. The *Rebecca* story belonged to each woman, but the mistake was to assume that therefore it was their own. The problem articulated in *Rebecca* as to a woman's lack of identity, echoed in the court proceedings over priority, took a new turn as Daphne travelled by boat to New York for the trial. As she opened the door of her cabin to see for the first time the figure of her publisher's wife Ellen Doubleday, she knew she was in love. If the whole of the build up to the trial had been focused around the question 'Who is the woman?', the true one, the real author, as she stared at Ellen these uncertainties became crystallised in the idea 'This is the woman.' What better moment for this great romance with a woman to begin: just as *Rebecca* is framed by the place of one woman who is more 'complete' than the heroine, now Daphne can describe Ellen as 'the complete woman I have never been'.

She saw Ellen, she said, as Mary Stuart and then as Rebecca herself. Whatever she wrote, she wanted to send it to her, like 'a child thrusting a bunch of daisies into its mother's hands'. At the same time that she is imagining what it would be like to be Ellen's daughter, she has violent dreams of attacking her own mother. And no sooner had Ellen appeared then Daphne split her object in two: while she elaborates a loving, idealising relation with her Lady, she also begins a sexual affair with another woman, the very person who had played the part based on Ellen's character in her play *Mother*, Gertrude Lawrence. And as Daphne declares that Ellen is a mother for her, the one she always wanted, she also says that she wants to be mother for Gertrude. All these mothers everywhere! And all of this starting at the time of the *Rebecca* trial. Why did Daphne entertain both relationships at this time? Why wasn't one enough? It would seem that Gertrude takes on her value as stepping into the place of Ellen, so that Ellen could be idealised and Gertrude slept with. But things are more complex. Gertrude had in fact once played opposite Daphne's father and was, in her words, 'the last of Daddy's actress loves'. She had played the music hall actress he marries in one production and his mistress in another. Surprising Gertrude one day clad only in bra and girdle, she suddenly saw the truth of what her father had once explained to her: the difference between the women men marry and the women they don't. The splitting in her love life was thus borrowed from a man: the sudden revelation showed that if these women had any relation with the image of the mother, this was not the fundamental point. What mattered was less the question of who she desired than that of the place *from which* she desired: which, as the example shows, was Gerald's. The perspective point which she assumed to be her own was her own, but it was equally that of someone else.

A transitory symptom in a young woman provides both a further illustration of this principle and a complication to its logic. At work one day, a female colleague confronts her in the Ladies and confesses that she is having an affair with her partner. She declares her authentic love for this man, and proceeds, in the heat of the moment, to evoke the sexual pleasure which he had provided her with: 'He made me come with his fingers,' she says. Shocked, the young woman returns home, and she and her partner talk. He swears love for her and says that he feels guilty and ashamed about his affair: it will never happen again, he insists, and he begs her forgiveness. A couple of days later a peculiar thing happens. She finds that her right hand is beginning to tingle, to such an extent that she finds it increasingly difficult to use it. The symptom continues, and it is only once the connection is made with the scene at work in which she heard the words 'He made me come with his fingers' that it disappears.

Now, one might wish to interpret this sequence as an act of defence on her part: if a hand cannot be used, a hand cannot be used to make someone else come. But it shows something more precise, indexed by the quality of 'tingling' in the hand, which indicates a sexual value: the tingling hands are those of the man, used to carry out the masturbatory activity. Her own perspective point is thus the perspective point of another, which leads to the much more profound problem at stake here. It would be false to conclude an analysis of this vignette with the proposition that the young woman identified with a man. Although the idea in itself is not false, what really needs to be asked is, What did the identification come into the place of? Spotting an identification with a man doesn't explain why a man might be identified with, and in this case the hurtful quality of the rival's exclamation 'He made me come with his fingers' covers over the most obvious fact: he made her come with his fingers because he couldn't do it any other way. The identification is thus an identification not just with man but with man as impotent, as castrated, man defined as lacking something.

This shows the real problem of identification. It is not always difficult to notice some identificatory trait – a gesture, a mannerism – but it is by no means simple to understand the logic in which the identification is situated. The fact that someone identifies introduces the question of *why* they have identified: an identification is not the solution to a problem, it is a way of articulating a problem. When Charlotte Brontë went off to Brussels to study and teach in the establishment of Mr Heger, a special relationship developed between the two of them, which some critics have chosen to call a love affair. Indeed, in each of her four novels a woman is loved by a man, and in no less than three of them the trigger is a piece of student writing, just like those that Charlotte would have produced for Mr Heger. He would encourage her in the development of her work, much to the displeasure of Mrs Heger, and once Charlotte was back in England at Haworth, it was exactly the relation Mr Heger–Charlotte that she reiterated with her sisters. It was now she who encouraged them and decided on the plans for the publication of their verses. If her odd behaviour on returning to the family home can be explained in terms of an identification with Heger, there is the real question of why the identification was set up in the first place. It was clearly of some importance for her, since it was only now that she could 'give up' her brother Branwell, neither informing him of nor including him in her publication projects. As with the clinical example we discussed earlier, the noting of an identification opens up to the question of its reasons: What was it responding to? And what were the conditions that made it possible?

Although the connections which allow the production of symptoms are unconscious, they may sometimes become clear quite suddenly outside the context of a psychoanalysis. We have had examples already with the mountain ranges of Rebecca West and the melody of Billie Whitelaw, and such revelations imply that something must be going on to allow the link to be made, a readiness which must have its own conditions. Although such insights are rare, the same question is introduced each time we remember a dream. Assuming that most of our dreams are never remembered or quickly forgotten, we have to ask why it is that from time to time we do recall the narrative of a dream or just a fragment, particularly if it concerns painful material. Again there must be a readiness to remember which is by no means always present. When connections are made and psychological issues seem to be simple enough, another quite different set of activities might be at play. If Rebecca

West and Billie Whitelaw had made the links they did and the feelings of uneasiness and sadness had *not* gone away, they may have supposed another, more hidden connection. A man became greatly troubled after seeing a film of a Zola novel in which a husband shrinks from intercourse with his wife for fear that in his sexual frenzy he might strangle her. When the man then reproduces this situation in his own marriage bed, he goes to see his GP, who refers him to a psychoanalyst, explaining that he has obviously identified with the would-be murderer. But, as the psychoanalyst noticed, if the important identification was really with the husband, the patient would not have become conscious of it. In other words, if there was an unconscious identification at play it was not with the husband but with the endangered wife.

After discussing this case, Bergler applies the same logic to one of the most famous pre-Freudian descriptions of the Oedipus complex. Stendhal's 1835 confession that he would have very much liked to sleep with his mother and do away with his father becomes less a crystal-clear description of a normally unconscious complex than a secondary product: the candour and insight of the confession obscure the real question of why Stendhal was allowed to become conscious of this at all. For Bergler, the answer lies not in the Oedipus complex but in its negative: the deeper set of wishes, he thinks, concerned hostility to the mother and a passive, feminine relation to the father. One may well criticise Bergler's model of the human psyche here. As in the rest of his work, there's the assumption that there are deeper and deeper layers of the psyche, each one being 'truer' than the others. His layered conception suggests that, for him, the unconscious is structured like a coffee cake, whereas for Lacan, in his famous formula, it has the structure of a language. Nonetheless, the basic question remains a valid one,